Digital Revolutionaries

The Men and Women Who
Brought Computing to Life

A **New York Times** BOOK

Digital Revolutionaries

The Men and Women Who Brought Computing to Life

STEVE LOHR

ROARING BROOK PRESS
NEW YORK

Jacket design by Christian Fuenfhausen
Book design by Michelle Gengaro-Kokmen

Cataloging-in-Publication Data is on file at the Library of Congress.

ISBN: 978-1-59643-532-2

Roaring Brook Press books are available for special promotions
and premiums. For details contact: Director of Special Markets,
Holtzbrinck Publishers.

Printed in August 2009 in the United States of America by
RR Donnelley & Sons Company, Harrisonburg, Virginia
First Edition October 2009
1 3 5 7 9 10 8 6 4 2

Digital Revolutionaries

The Men and Women Who Brought Computing to Life

*For Nikki, to give her a glimpse of the people
and technology behind her Web site.*

Contents

1

New Geeks and Nemo

Ever wonder how computers work? What goes on behind the screen and the keyboard? If so, you share important traits with the pioneers of the digital revolution. Curiosity and a sense of determination to push beyond the limits of the current technology are qualities these computer revolutionaries embody. Without their questioning minds, we might still have the room-sized computing machines of the 1940s instead of today's microcomputers. Cars might not have become the computers on wheels they are now, and we might not be able to download an MP3 file to a laptop and transfer it to an iPod. Would the iPod even exist? For every technological puzzle that begs to be solved, there is a computing "geek" who will try to solve it simply because it is there.

Long before people were called computer nerds, Charles Simonyi was one, as a teenager in Budapest in the 1960s. Things were very different back then. Computers didn't play music or movies. They were big machines, and they were scarce. In Communist Hungary, the government owned most computers and, through a family friend, Simonyi got an unpaid job in the computer center of a government agency. As a child, he had always been interested in mechanical things. He loved Erector sets, but parts were often hard to get in Hungary, so he built imaginary machines with the pieces he could get.

The government computer Simonyi worked on had no mouse and no screen with easy-to-use graphic icons like the kind we point to and then click to make today's personal computers

2

perform tasks. To instruct the Russian-made mainframe to do anything, Simonyi had to master the arcane art of speaking to the computer in a language understood by the machine: programming code. It was frustrating at first, but Simonyi had a real knack for it, and he was thrilled that he could program the computer to do everything from calculating statistical plans for the government to playing games of tic-tac-toe and chess for fun. "In a way, I found my ultimate Erector set—an Erector set without limits," he recalled.

Simonyi was a strong-willed young man and an independent thinker. He despised the restraints on individual freedom under communism, and his computer skills would serve as his passport to the West. At seventeen, he left for a temporary job in Denmark, but he had no plans to return. His parents knew of his intention, and the consequences. He would not see his family again for more than twenty years. Simonyi arrived in Denmark with no money and few possessions. Still, he had a job and talents that would grow and become increasingly valuable over the years.

Simonyi emigrated to California as a student, attending the University of California at Berkeley and then earning a doctorate at Stanford University. He always worked doing computer jobs on the side to pay his way. In the 1970s, he was a researcher at the Xerox Palo Alto Research Center, a hothouse of ideas that later found their way into successful products.

In 1980, Simonyi showed up at a fledgling company outside Seattle: Microsoft. His reputation and work at the Xerox research center got him an immediate job offer from Bill Gates, and Simonyi became one of the early employees at Microsoft. At the Xerox lab, Simonyi had developed an innovative program for creating documents that made it possible for words to be typed in all sorts of sizes and styles, and for graphics to be inserted on the screen. At Microsoft, Simonyi's ideas were put into Microsoft Word, the writing and editing program that is one of the most widely used software products in the world.

When I visited Simonyi a few years ago, we met at his house, a striking modern home of glass, steel, and wood that sweeps down a hillside to the edge of Lake Washington, near Seattle. His house has its own library, fitness center, swimming pool, and computer lab. On the walls hang original works by modern artists like Roy Lichtenstein and Jasper Johns. Besides art, Simonyi collects jets. He has two, including a NATO fighter jet, which he flies. He's even flown to the International Space Station as a

Charles Simonyi floats during a parabolic flight aboard a zero-gravity simulator in preparation for his flight in space.

Techno-Dwellings House Cyber-Egos of the Rich

Continued From Page 1

James wrote, one could hear "something like the chink of money itself in the murmur of the breezy little waves."

In Woodside, a musk-and-manure enclave where "Equestrian Crossing" signs dot leafy byways, the sheer size of Xanadus like the 18,000-square-foot château that A.C.

Jim Wilson/The New York Times

Charles Simonyi's bachelor home on Lake Washington is so vast that a visitor can feel like a lonely asteroid rattling around the solar system.

Techno-Dwellings for the Cyber-Egos of the Mega-Rich

By PATRICIA LEIGH BROWN

MEDINA, Wash. — Some chilly nights, after his computer turns off every light bulb, the fireplace and the infrared heat over the patio, and before it adjusts the blinds, Charles Simonyi, Microsoft's chief programming wizard, stands on a cantilevered terrace of his 20,500-square-foot lake-side home here, marveling at what he calls "the absolute magic," the quiet perfection of it all.

To the southwest is Mercer Island, where a co-founder of Microsoft, Paul Allen, has built a Scandinavian-inspired compound with 74,000 square feet of buildings including an indoor basketball court, a recording studio, an office tower and a made-to-order grotto.

To the northwest is the Gates House, the most famous $30 million, 45,000-square-foot construction site in the world. Ensconced in its hillside like the funerary temple of Hatshepsut, this oasis-in-progress has already become a public showpiece for the Bill Gates legend (buy the book, tour it on CD-ROM). It is the techno-future at its grandest; guests will enter a dazzling reception hall lined with 24 video monitors, each with a 40-inch picture tube. Don't even try keeping up with the Gateses.

The nerds are nesting. Like William K. Vanderbilt, whose turn-of-the-century "cottage" in Newport, R.I., was inspired by Louis XIV, they have been gripped with "la manie de bâtir," the fever to build. And like those prolific house-raising robber barons, today's cyber-barons are engaged in acts of conspicuous construction. Few would call them architectural taste makers. But they are turning affluent communities like Medina, outside Seattle — not far from Microsoft's headquarters in Redmond — and Woodside and Atherton in Silicon Valley into born-again Newports. There, as Henry

Continued on Page 39, Column 1

TECHNO-MACHO The mansion of T. J. Rodgers in Woodside, Calif., overlooking his vineyard and winery. Palm trees are his addition.

GREEK REVIVAL Joe Vetter's amphitheater, inspired by one in ancient Epidaurus. "Building something around themselves is an experience people want to have."

IMPERIAL CONTROL T. J. Rodgers at the helm in his home theater in Silicon Valley. A computer panel lets him display films on high-definition monitors throughout his 4,500-square-foot house.

Charles Simonyi's home was profiled in The New York Times *on August 4, 1996, along with the compounds of other technology moguls.*

space tourist. He has made multimillion-dollar philanthropic donations to Oxford University, the Institute of Advanced Study in Princeton, and elsewhere. He is a billionaire, and he owes it all to his extraordinary ability to talk to computers in the language of programming code— along with good timing and good fortune.

His life story personifies the rise of modern computing over the past fifty years, as it evolved from a lab experiment to a huge, rich industry, and from a technology for an elite few to one used by everyone. Even today, Simonyi thinks computers are still far too difficult for ordinary people to program. The computer revolution, he insists, is just getting underway.

Still, Simonyi cannot help but marvel at the pace of progress in a few decades, a very short time in the sweep of history. "Even with the primitive tools we use, look at how much computing can do," he observed. "It's amazing."

It's ironic that computers, developed by independent thinkers and revolutionaries, have become so commonplace, so much a part of the fabric of everyday life, that they often go unnoticed, as if hiding in plain sight. You may not see them, but chances are, they're there. They surround us—not just personal computers at home and school, but also cell phones, handheld music players, televisions, kitchen appliances, and supermarket cash registers are computing devices of one kind or another. Cars rely as much on software and semiconductors as on gears and pistons these days. The list goes on and on.

Not so long ago, however, computers were rare things, indeed. At the dawn of modern computing in the 1940s and 1950s, computers were hulking room-sized machines. They required teams of white-suited scientists to keep them up and running. The scientists fixed them by prowling around inside the machine, seeing where some wire had come loose and plugging it into the correct circuit by hand. Yet one of those room-sized mechanical behemoths could not match the computing power of a single microchip no larger than the tip of your finger today.

As computers have become smaller, their influence has become greater and greater. Almost anywhere you look, the impact of computing is being felt, more so all the time, and often in ways we don't fully appreciate. We take e-mail, instant messages, and Web-based social networks, such as Facebook, for granted. Yet these computing tools subtly shape how we communicate and deal with each other.

In one field after another, computing plays

The ENIAC computer was a system of switches and vacuum tubes that occupied an entire room. Here, a technician programs the computer to perform a calculation in 1946.

an increasing role. In medicine, for example, if you get an injury playing soccer or basketball that could be serious, chances are the doctor will take a picture of the inside of the injured arm or leg. Those images are captured, refined, and analyzed using computer technology. Only in the last decade has the use of that medical imaging technology become routine. In biology, another science transformed by computing, human genome research seeks to explore the mysteries of life based on the understanding that DNA, which carries our genetic information, is much like computer code. The machine code that a computer processes is digital, ones and zeros, while there are four chemical building blocks in DNA, designated A, G, C, and T. Humans, to be sure, are not computers. But there are some profound similarities: Humans process coded genetic information, while computers process digital information in code.

Computer-generated simulations are vital tools in the hunt for new drugs, in oil exploration, economic modeling, and weather prediction. These simulations are much like "The Sims" computer game, where assumptions about "cyberpeople" on the screen—what they do and how they spend their time—determine how a virtual city unfolds.

In drug discovery, the molecular structure of experimental compounds and how they might interact in the body are simulated. In oil exploration, the known geologic information about rock formations, heat, and pressure is fed into computers to create an underground picture to suggest where, thousands of years ago, oil might have formed—and thus where to drill. In economics, computer simulations are used to predict how people and markets might behave if the price or supply of goods is changed. Early warnings of global warming came from a NASA climate scientist, based on his computer simulations.

Our popular culture runs on computers, from music to movies. In Hollywood, when a director needs a killer storm, the Roman Coliseum, King Kong, flesh-eating raptors, or a superhero-caliber stunt, it's no problem. All those and much more have been conjured up to frighten and thrill thanks to the magic of computer-generated special effects.

Computing has also permanently changed the practice of politics. The Web is a democratic, bottom-up technology that resists control. A Web log, or blog, can be created by anyone with a personal computer, access to the Internet, and a little skill. In a democracy, such as the United States, bloggers represent a new voice in the nation's political debate. But the authorities in places like China play a constant cat-and-mouse game with political bloggers, shutting down blogs that then pop up again a short time later. Blog posts can be mean-spirited or untrue, but they can also be insightful and uncover new information. Politicians, newspapers, and television networks all must pay attention to what is being said in the "blogosphere"—another computing innovation.

The benefits are many. When a friend moves

to another state or another country, thanks to the Internet we can easily stay in touch in a way that was unimaginable in the days of paper letters sent by regular mail, delivered days or weeks after they were written. But the convenience and immediacy of Internet communications doesn't come free. There is a cost, or at least a social risk. A thoughtless remark, an insult, or a lie can last a long time in an e-mail message, on a blog or on a Web site posting, souring a friendship, tarnishing someone's reputation, or worse. The same words, if spoken, might be missed or quickly forgotten.

All tools can be used for good or ill. A hammer can be used to build a house or as a weapon. It depends not on the tool but on the person using it. The same is true, of course, of computer tools. The Internet, for example, makes it easy to reach out and touch someone. But when we do reveal ourselves to others, we become increasingly accessible to strangers. Still, the computer and the global computer network, the Internet, are universal tools—their uses limited mainly by the imagination of the people using and programming them. Luckily for us, those computer scientists whose imagination propels technology forward are eager to envision the possible uses for these tools and work to develop the hardware and software even before they have an exact map of how. They lead technology more often than not.

Computer science is not just for engineers anymore. Today's technologists can be found in medicine, law, media, and the arts as well as all the sciences. These "new geeks" are a world apart from the old stereotype of the computer nerd as a cubicle drone more comfortable with machines than with people.

Kira Lehtomaki is one of these young technologists. For her, the appeal of computing was art, not science. Art projects, not computers, were her childhood passion. And when, as a three-year-old, she first saw a videotape of the Disney film *Sleeping Beauty*, she decided what she wanted to do when she grew up. She wanted to be one of those artists who stirred life into the animated characters in movies using pencils, paper, and imagination—an animator.

The dreams of most three-year-olds are soon forgotten, but not Kira's. Growing up, she drew constantly, studied art, and read all the books she could find on animation and how it was done at the Walt Disney Company. Disney created animated movies, starting with *Snow White and the Seven Dwarfs* in 1937, and defined the art form for the next sixty years with classics ranging from *Pinocchio* and *Dumbo* to *Beauty and the Beast* and *The Lion King*. One summer, Kira even took a job at Disneyland in southern California as a "cookie artist"—painting designs and Mickey Mouse faces—because that job allowed her to spend a couple of days watching how things were done at Disney's animation studio.

The Disney tradition was the pencil-and-paper way. But by the late 1990s, hand-drawn animation was being challenged by something new—computer generated animation. Kira resisted the new technology at first, but was won over when, as a nineteen-year-old college

A still from the classic Disney film, Snow White and the Seven Dwarfs, *released in 1937. Traditional animation required that each frame of the film be drawn by hand and then transferred to an animation cell.*

student, she saw *Monsters Inc.* in 2001, the fourth feature film from the pioneer of computer animation, Pixar Animation Studios.

"I was just blown away," she recalled, by the range of expression and movement in the buddy film, as the hulking, hairy Sulley and his one-eyed sidekick, Mike, led a benevolent revolt at their scream factory.

Kira took up computer graphics in college. And at twenty-three, she was a researcher at the University of Washington's animation labs in Seattle and traveling regularly to Northern

Computer technology adds layers of detail, creating images with greater depth and motion, as in this scene from Monsters, Inc., *released by Pixar in 2001.*

California to train with the animators at Pixar. "These two worlds of art and computing are really merging, and, if anything, they will blend even more," she observed. (Kira later became an animator for Disney, and her first credit was for the movie *Bolt* in 2008.)

Some years ago, I spent several days at Pixar's waterfront offices along the San Francisco Bay. The people and corporate culture of Pixar show how computer technology is spreading and evolving into hybrids of computing and something else—in this case, art and entertainment. Pixar was founded and built by people who deeply understood that computers were powerful creative tools instead of merely big number-crunching calculators. They sustained their belief for years, when many others doubted. And they were proven right, again and again. For its part, Disney was so impressed by Pixar's track record that it bought the company in early 2006 for more than seven billion dollars. Yet the Pixar sale was essentially a reverse takeover: Pixar's leaders were put in charge of overseeing Disney's animation studio, which had fallen behind.

When I visited Pixar, it was clear the place was designed to encourage creativity and fun. The hallways were marked with blue plastic signs bearing names like Toy Boulevard and Scooter Run. In fact, workers periodically zipped by on white scooters, ringing bicycle bells. Animators and artists worked in partitioned cubicles, each decorated differently and each lit by the glow from a computer screen.

Old couches, lava lamps, Art Deco mirrors,

and Japanese screens were all part of the mix. Playful artillery fire—from Nerf ball bazookas—whizzed by. Humor was in the air. For his telephone message, Andrew Stanton, the codirector of *A Bug's Life*, who would later direct *Finding Nemo* and *Wall-E*, spoke in a mock Eastern European accent, with eerie music playing in the background: "This is Andrew Stanton's psychic hotline. Since I already know why you're calling, you can hang up at the sound of the beep."

The head of Pixar's creative team was John Lasseter, a former Disney animator. He grew up in Whittier, California, a short ride from the Disneyland theme park in Anaheim. As a teenager, he worked as a boat skipper on the Jungle Cruise. Disney blood, Lasseter often says, runs through his veins.

Lasseter's office had the look of a cluttered child's room. A gumball machine stood beside his desk. Big boxes of Cheerios™ and Lucky Charms™ cluttered the desktop. A collection of vintage toys—original versions of Mr. Potato

Head™, Slinky™, and others—rested on a shelf. Lasseter, a round-faced man with oval glasses, wore a short-sleeved shirt adorned with cartoon characters. He took a child's delight in showing off his toys. "Isn't that one great?" he said, pointing to a favorite.

Yet entertainment is also a serious matter to Lasseter. And he has obviously given the subject a lot of serious thought and study over the years. Technical innovation, Lasseter said, has always been used in Hollywood to create illusion and dramatic effect. He pointed to the innovative lighting, angles, and shots used by director Alfred Hitchcock in classic movies like *The Man Who Knew Too Much*, *Rear Window*, and *Vertigo*. Walt Disney himself, Lasseter noted, pushed the technology of his time to the limits in making *Snow White* and the animated movies that followed. Until then, animation was largely an arcade novelty—people paid to look in a viewer and watch drawings flip quickly past to simulate a few seconds of action, like a clown falling down. "But Walt Disney made that arcade novelty into an art form," Lasseter said. "And here, we've brought computer animation out of the realm of science into an art form."

A skilled artist, Lasseter studied hand-drawn animation at the California Institute of the Arts, and he worked at Disney's animation studio for five years. He was helping to animate *Mickey's Christmas Carol*, drawing Goofy, Donald, and Scrooge McDuck, when he saw *Tron*, a 1982 science-fiction film with early computer-animated special effects. He was amazed, not so much by what he saw then but by the moviemaking potential of computer graphics—the power of computing to add another dimension to animation, a step beyond the flat, two dimensions of hand-drawn images into a 3-D world. "You can create a world," he explained. "It isn't real but it is more real than animated films ever could be before, and it makes it easier to bring the audience into that world."

But Disney was not really interested in computer animation, and Lasseter's fascination with the technology mystified the old

Disney crowd at the time. "He was all gung-ho for computers even though he drew very, very well," recalled Frank Thomas, one of the great, early Disney animators. "The computer images were very crude and stiff in those days, but John Lasseter saw where things were going."

An early glimpse of the future came in Lasseter's 1986 animated short film, *Luxor Jr.* Lasseter chose as his subject an object near at hand, an architect's lamp sitting on his desk. He moved it around, used it as his model and the resulting animated short film told the story of a spirited little lamp playing with a ball, a father lamp, a child's disappointment when a ball is deflated, and fresh hope when a new one rolls into view. The range of movement and emotion in the animation of the little jumping lamp was an eye-opening display of the potential of computer animation. Two years later, Lasseter won an Academy Award for another animated short, *Tin Toy*.

However impressive artistically, the short films brought in no money. And as a company,

Pixar was struggling to stay afloat. The technology and expertise needed to create a full-length feature film were still years away. In the meantime, Pixar tried to earn its way by producing animated commercials and selling specialized computers that did things like sharpen the images photographed by American spy satellites.

The acclaimed animated short films were back-office projects, done on tight budgets by Lasseter and a couple of others. "I slept under my desk to finish the shorts," he recalled. The short films proved to be Pixar's salvation. Disney admired them, and in its first link with the young studio, agreed to distribute and help finance Pixar's feature films, starting with *Toy Story* in 1995. It was the first feature-length computer-animated movie.

A Pixar production requires both creative skill and technological firepower. A film typically takes three or four years from inception to opening in theaters, while computer technology improves at a relentless pace, doubling in speed every two years. So each Pixar movie represents a bet on what can be accomplished artistically by pushing the limits of computing in a future that has not yet arrived. Crowd scenes or chase scenes, for example, that would have been impossible when computer-animated movie development began, have become technically achievable. "You have to have a pioneering spirit to do this," Lasseter said, "because we bite off more than we can chew every time."

The eclectic team assembled at Pixar is the main reason the studio's bets have paid off. "What makes it all work," Lasseter said, "is the wacky, interesting collection of talented people here. The place is a unique blend of Hollywood and Silicon Valley."

If Lasseter is Hollywood, then Ed Catmull, Pixar's president, is Silicon Valley. Catmull is the company's technology mastermind and leader. Quiet, bespectacled, and soft-spoken, he is a star in computer graphics circles and the owner of three Academy Awards for technical achievement.

Growing up in Salt Lake City, Catmull saw *Pinocchio* and *Peter Pan*, and dreamed of being an animator at Disney one day. But math and science, not art, were his gifts. At the University of Utah, he studied physics and computer science as an undergraduate and later earned a Ph.D. in computer science. At Utah, Catmull discovered techniques for adding texture, depth, and curves to images on computer screens. In 1973, he made his first 3-D animation—a likeness of his left hand that could be rotated and viewed from all angles. The hand animation got noticed in Hollywood, and even found its way into a science-fiction movie in 1976, *Futureworld*. At the time, computer graphics had the primitive look of science projects. But Catmull was convinced the technology had great potential.

A computer-animated feature film is among the most daunting challenges in modern computing. Pixar's technical ranks are loaded with computer scientists from leading universities. "The kind of people who work here, in an earlier time, would probably have been involved in something like putting a man on the moon," Catmull said. "They are people who hunger to solve huge new challenges and want to make an impact on the world and on culture."

Yet Pixar's technical magic, at its best, goes unnoticed. "You want what is on the screen to be drop-dead beautiful," he explained, "and not have the audience think about how it's done."

Poppa and Peanut Butter Sandwiches

It may seem like magic, but a computer-generated movie is the result of art, science, and high-tech factory work. And what you see on the screen is made possible by decades of steady progress in computing, as well as mathematical concepts that reach back for centuries.

The early work on a Pixar computer-animated movie is little different from a hand-drawn film. That is a matter of imagining a story, writing a script, drawing storyboards, choosing the music, and selecting actors, who, in an animated movie, are the voices of the characters.

The art department's drawings of characters, sets, and props are either sculpted by hand and scanned into the computer or modeled in 3-D directly into the computer. The characters and objects are each equipped with the software equivalent of hinges, so the animator can make them move. A character's face might have more than one hundred such digital hinges.

The animators take over next. They create the body language and emotions for characters. Animators are keen observers of human movement and expression, noticing details most people miss. "Everybody waits differently," one Pixar animator noted. Bringing the character to life on screen is painstaking work, using a keyboard and mouse, sometimes a digital tablet and pen. Manipulating the on-screen character to get just the right effect, an animator resembles a high-tech puppeteer.

Then comes a process known as shading. It is done with software programs that allow for intricate variations in color and texture, a breeze rippling Sulley's fur in *Monsters, Inc.*, for example. Next, the digital lighting is added with software that automatically adjusts the light level with each movement of an object or character, like the water-refracted light that glistens on Nemo as he swims. The result is a level of detail and realism that is beyond the reach of hand-drawn animation, no matter how much "pencil mileage"—coloring and shading by hand—is used.

The last step in production is to translate all the data in the digital files that make up a shot—sets, color, characters, movement, and light—into a single frame of film. This rendering is done in what amounts to a high-tech power plant, a supercomputer center. Each frame represents one twenty-fourth of a second of screen time. Rendering that eye's blink worth of movie time can take hours in the computer engine room.

On the screen, we see bright colors, subtle movements, and expressions of anger, sadness, or delight. The computers behind these cinematic works of art see none of that. The computer's language is digital—binary digits, or bits, ones and zeros. That is how a computer sees the world, as strings of ones and zeros, representing tiny electronics switches that are on or off.

Software bridges the gap between what we see and what the machine sees. Software is the translator between man and machine, conveying our questions or orders to the computers that surround us. It is software—the embodiment of human intelligence—that makes a computer do anything useful, interesting, or entertaining. Behind the images of a 3-D movie, the sounds of an iPod music player, or even the letters that appear on your computer screen when you type on the keyboard is software, translating everything down to the ones and zeros the machine understands.

In most software programs these days, the translation progresses using thousands or millions of lines of instruction to the machine. Layer after layer of programming code is required to move up from the machine-level communication to something a human user wants to see, hear, or use.

The computer-graphics software used in Hollywood or in games, for example, builds three-dimensional shapes layer by layer. It works almost like a computerized version of the old connect-the-dot pictures in coloring books. The software program first stores the data points of an object's outline and shape. Next, it draws lines that connect the points, then the surfaces defined by the lines, and assembles those surfaces again and again and again into the likeness of a toy, a fish, a face, or whatever.

In software, the step-by-step set of instructions for doing something is called an algorithm. Computer programming is often compared to cooking, and an algorithm can be thought of as the mathematical equivalent of a recipe. If the program were "Peanut Butter Sandwich," the algorithmic instructions might be: Unscrew lid from jar. Dip knife in peanut butter. Spread evenly on slice of bread. Put second slice of bread on top. Slice sandwich in half.

Computing is a close cousin of mathematics, and the algorithm is a bedrock principle in both. The term itself goes back 1,200 years and comes from the family name of a ninth-century Persian mathematician and astronomer, Muhammad ibn Mūsā al-Khwārizmī. Modern computing is sort of like math on steroids, a technology originally used for rapid calculations in science and engineering whose impact has spread broadly across society.

Even the early computer theorists had large ambitions for the machines they envisioned. In the nineteenth century, the English mathematician Charles Babbage drew up elaborate designs for his Analytical Engine, a machine he never built but a conceptual forerunner of the modern computer. And in 1936, the British mathematician Alan Turing introduced the notion of a "universal machine," which could, in theory, simulate the work of any computing device, including the human brain.

Yet Babbage and Turing never built their machines. As impressive as their ideas were, they remained just ideas. It was not until World

War II that electronics had advanced to the point that building useful computers became a real possibility. Electricity was vital to modern computing for two reasons—it brought speed and flexibility. Advances in the ability to control the flow of electrons through complex circuitry in machines were also essential. And by World War II, electrical engineering had progressed enough to open the door to electronic computers. To be sure, smart people have solved thorny problems using mechanical calculating devices through the ages (think of the abacus), but the process was never speedy. The calculations used to calibrate the thermonuclear reaction inside the atomic bomb, for example, were done by row after row of men and women working on hand-cranked mechanical calculators. It was a slow, painstaking process.

Electricity is fast, traveling in theory at the speed of light, 186,000 miles a second. That's seven times around the Earth's equator in a second. Inside a machine, over tiny copper wires, the actual speed of electricity is slower, perhaps half or even a third the theoretical speed. But it's still really fast.

Electricity meant that the underlying language of computing would be a binary code. Electricity is inherently binary because it has two natural states, on or off. As it turns out, a binary code—with two elements—is both remarkably simple and powerful. For example, Morse code, developed by Samuel Morse in the nineteenth century for telegraph messages, is a binary code; each letter in the alphabet is represented by a different pattern of dots and dashes. In our computers today, each letter or number is represented by a different pattern of eight bits, ones and zeros. There are eight bits in a byte; a megabyte is a million bytes, and a gigabyte is a billion bytes.

Electricity flows through circuits that are switched on or off. Circuits can be linked by wires in almost endless arrays these days. Electrical impulses and on/off signals can be stored, amplified and relayed, and manipulated and translated by clever software.

The computers of today are the result of a steady stream of inventions over the years in new materials, hardware design, and software. But the door was opened with the arrival of the electronic digital computer, a technology that would begin to translate the ideas of Charles Babbage and Alan Turing into reality.

The machine generally credited with starting the era of digital electronic computing was the ENIAC. It was a computer experiment started by the United States Army during World War II to try to reduce one of the tragedies of war—soldiers mistakenly killed by inaccurately fired artillery shells from their own side, known as *friendly fire*. Lives could be saved if long-range artillery fire could be aimed more accurately using more precise calculations of the flight path of shells, the angle of firing, and the effect of crosswinds. The task was assigned to the ENIAC, short for Electronic Numerical Integrator and Computer. The ENIAC proved a success, though it was not completed until 1946, after World War II was over.

Electronic Computer Figures Like a Flash

NEW ALL-ELECTRONIC COMPUTER AND ITS INVENTORS

Continued From Page 1

which they will witness the Eniac in action at the Moore School of Electrical Engineering, where it was built with the assistance of the Army Ordnance Department.

The Eniac was invented and perfected by two young scientists of the school, Dr. John William Mauchly, 38, a physicist and amateur meteorologist, and his associate, J. Presper Eckert Jr., 26, chief engineer of the project. Assistance also was given by many others at the school.

Army ordnance men had been on the lookout for a machine with which to prepare a large volume of

Electronic Computer Flashes Answers, May Speed Engineering

By T. R. KENNEDY Jr.
Special to THE NEW YORK TIMES.

PHILADELPHIA, Feb. 14—One of the war's top secrets, an amazing machine which applies electronic speeds for the first time to mathematical tasks hitherto too difficult and cumbersome for solution, was announced here tonight by the War Department. Leaders who saw the device in action for the first time heralded it as a tool with which to begin, to rebuild scientific affairs on new foundations.

Such instruments, it was said, could revolutionize modern engineering, bring on a new epoch of industrial design, and eventually eliminate much slow and costly trial-and-error development work now deemed necessary in the fashioning of intricate machines. Heretofore, sheer mathematical difficulties have often forced designers to accept inferior solutions of their problems, with higher costs and slower progress.

The "Eniac," as the new elec-

tronic speed marvel is known, virtually eliminates time in doing such jobs. Its inventors say it computes a mathematical problem 1,000 times faster than it has ever been done before.

The machine is being used on a problem in nuclear physics.

The Eniac, known more formally as "the electronic numerical integrator and computer," has not a single moving mechanical part. Nothing inside its 18,000 vacuum tubes and several miles of wiring moves except the tiniest elements of matter-electrons. There are, however, mechanical devices associated with it which translate or "interpret" the mathematical language of man to terms understood by the Eniac, and vice versa.

Ceremonies dedicating the machine will be held tomorrow night at a dinner given by a group of Government and scientific men at the University of Pennsylvania, after

3, Column 3

paring the machine to solve a hydrodynamical ...puters hitherto have required weeks to perform. ...room 30 by 60 feet and weighs thirty tons. It ...t 200,000 man-hours of work.

in 1941, hoping he might be able to realize his ambition, to revolutionize the art of dealing with huge numbers in complex form. He believed, for instance, that something could be done about long-range weather predicting.

In the field of peacetime activities Dr. Mauchly foresees not only better weather-predicting—months ahead—but also better airplanes, gas turbines, micro-wave radio tubes, television, prime movers, projectiles operating at supersonic speeds carrying cargoes in peace and even more and better aeronautics in studying the movements of the planets.

According to Colonel Goldstine, "mountainous" computational burdens have been carried by scientists in the past, which will be largely removed by electronic computers. He pointed out that the solution of equations of motion has been a hindrance in the past and that studies of shell flight, high-speed planes, rockets and bombs are "a few of the fields that will benefit hugely through electronic computing."

"...thought impossible because they might require a lifetime will be readily resolved for man's use.

"The old era is going, the new one of electronic speed is on the way, when we can begin all over again to tackle scientific problems with new understanding," he told reporters.

Mr. Eckert briefly described the Harvard and Massachusetts Institute of Technology mechanical and electro-mechanical computing machines, the most recent of which was announced only a few months ago.

...when the problem is put ...dly cards, they are dropped into a slot in a "reader." The man who wants the answers may then sit down and await results. He seldom has to wait long; the Eniac does most of its tasks in seconds.

A unit called "a master programmer" oversees the whole computation and makes sure it is carried out.

The Eniac has some 40 panels nine feet high, which bristle with control and indicating material. Pink neon lights blink on several panels as buttons are pressed. Numbers are printed beside the lights.

Those who witnessed the demonstration entered a 30-by 60-foot room. The computer took up most of the space.

Dr. Arthur W. Burks of the Moore School explained that the basic arithmetical operations, if made to take place rapidly enough, might in time solve almost any problem.

"Before You Can Say . . ."

"Watch closely, you may miss it," he asked, as a button was pressed to multiply 97,367 by itself 5,000 times. Most of the onlookers missed it—the operation took place in less than the wink of an eye.

To demonstrate the Eniac's extreme speed, Dr. Burks next slowed down the action by a factor of 1,000 and did the same problem. Had the visitors been content to

...by a trained man. The same ...it in exactly fifteen seconds.

All problems must first be resolved to their essentials, punched on cards and run through an International Business Machines unit called a "reader." The reader translates the mathematical language to that of the Eniac, and vice versa. When this is done the machine is ready to operate. Numerical values covering a wide

...went into the building of the machine. It contains more than half a million soldered joints, and cost about $400,000. Three times as much electricity is required to operate it as for one of our largest broadcasters—150 kilowatts.

Little more than three years ago the Eniac was only an idea; today it is perhaps the greatest marvel of electronic ingenuity. Dr. Mauchly joined the Moore School staff

The announcement in 1946 by the War Department of the electronic numerical integrator and computer (ENIAC) was chronicled by The New York Times.

But the ENIAC had to be programmed by hand. To prepare, the programmers would spend many days drawing elaborate charts on paper, mapping out how an artillery-firing calculation could most efficiently navigate its way through the ENIAC. Then, they had to properly plug a maze of wires one by one into circuits and carefully set row upon row of electrical switches. It was as if the machine had to be rebuilt for each new problem. It had no software.

A technician manipulates one of hundreds of dials on IBM's room-size ENIAC computer.

A real software breakthrough came in the 1950s—FORTRAN, short for FORmula TRANslator. It was a programming language designed for scientists and engineers, the people most likely to use computers in those days. FORTRAN, which resembled a combination of abbreviated English and algebra, was a computing language that looked very similar to the math formulas that scientists and engineers used daily in their work. FORTRAN moved communication with the computer up a level, closer to the human and away from the machine. That is why FORTRAN is called the first higher-level programming language. *(In 1967, John Backus wrote a* Times *article explaining FORTRAN. You can read it on page 127.)*

Much of the history of modern computing can be seen as a march along the road that began with FORTRAN, trying to open things up to more people and more uses, widening the impact of the technology. And the story of the FORTRAN project itself and the people involved offers a glimpse into the early days of the computer age.

John Backus, who led the FORTRAN team, followed a haphazard path into computer science. He grew up in an affluent family in Wilmington, Delaware, but his parents spent little time with him and he was often left on his own. As a child, Backus recalled, he enjoyed playing with a beloved chemistry set and fixing things, including a dilapidated motorbike that he repaired at twelve after a friend had given it up for dead. "I've always liked mechanical stuff," he said.

When I spoke to him, Backus was 76, retired, and still cheerfully puttering with gadgets, both digital and mechanical. He had rigged up the garage door and front gate of his home in San Francisco with automatic remote controls of his own design. He moderated a local online discussion group, and he had just purchased one of the first TiVo-style digital video recorders for skipping television commercials, searching through program listings, and recording favorite shows. "This is a great invention," Backus declared with enthusiasm. "It's going to change television."

As a kid, Backus was bright, but he was a wayward student. He was tossed out of one school after another. Recalling one private school, he said, "The delight of that place was all the rules you could break." After flunking out of college, Backus was drafted into the army in 1943. Stellar scores on army aptitude tests got him government-funded scholarships to a couple of universities.

The war ended in 1945, and while wondering what to do next, Backus decided that what his small apartment in New York needed was a good sound system. He began to construct his own high-fidelity set from scratch. To build an amplifier, Backus had to calculate points on the curve of sound waves, and he found wrestling with the mathematics oddly compelling. "It was so awful to do that calculation, but somehow it kind of got me interested in math," he remembered. Backus applied to Columbia University, which admitted him as a probationary student, given his decidedly mixed academic record. He did well at Columbia, completing a bachelor's degree and earning a master's in mathematics in 1950.

One spring day, shortly before he graduated from Columbia, Backus visited IBM®'s headquarters, which was in midtown Manhattan at the time. He had heard about the massive scientific calculating machine on display there, and he wanted to take a look at it. IBM had installed the computer on the first floor, behind large windows. With its thousands of flashing lights, clacking switches, punched cards shuffling, and paper tapes whirring, the computer was a tourist curiosity. (Electrical sensors, usually metal brushes, read the data coded as patterns of holes punched in the cards and tapes.) The passersby did not know what to make of the machine, but they soon dubbed it "Poppa."

Backus walked inside and was given a brief tour. When he told a woman he was about to get his master's degree in math, she immediately escorted him to see one of the inventors of the machine. Backus protested. "I wasn't wearing a tie, I had a hole in the sleeve of my jacket, and I didn't know anything really about computers," he recalled.

No matter. The IBM scientist asked him a few questions that Backus described as math

John Backus, inventor of the FORTRAN computer language, at home in San Francisco, California, in 2001.

"brain teasers" and hired him on the spot. As what? "As a programmer," he replied, shrugging. "That was the way it was done in those days," long before there was a discipline called "computer science" or schools teaching it.

The machine Backus saw at IBM's headquarters was the Selective Sequence Electronic Calculator, known as the Super Calculator. It was essentially an IBM science project built to let the company's researchers test the limits of electronic calculators and gain experience.

The Super Calculator was probably the most powerful computational machine of its day. *(You can read a* New York Times *article from the unveiling of the Super Calculator on page 123.)*

Backus got his introduction to programming on the Super Calculator. The giant machine had a fraction of the computing power found in an Apple iPod, let alone one of today's desktop personal computers. But that did not prevent the IBM researchers from using the hulking computer for large scientific calculations. Backus, for example, prepared a program to calculate the position of the moon and nearby planets at any time over the years, which required endless number crunching.

Yet the programming itself, Backus said, amounted to "hand-to-hand combat with the machine." The machine had to be agonizingly set up by hand for each program, flipping switches and plugging wires into circuits. Programs would run for weeks. Debugging was done by ear. Circuits were opened and closed by relays—metal bars attached to springs that were raised by the pulling force of electromagnets. The thousands of relays being slapped into position made a horrible racket. But to the trained ear, it was not merely random industrial noise. A repeated rhythm from one corner of the machine signified that a program was frozen in some calculating loop, as grating as listening to a scratched CD playing the same line from a song again and again. If we think, again, of a computer program as similar to the recipe for a peanut butter sandwich, it would be constantly repeating one instruction: "Unscrew lid from jar. Unscrew lid from jar . . ."

When a new generation of computer arrived, with mute electronic switches instead of mechanical relays, Backus felt a twinge of panic. "I wondered," he recalled, "how are we going to debug this enormous silent monster?"

This early programming required an intimate understanding of how the machine worked. Only a small group of people had the arcane skills and mysterious knowledge needed to speak to the machine, as if high priests in a primitive society. Backus was eager to speed things up and somehow simplify programming. "I figured there had to be a better way," he explained. "You simply had to make it easier for people to program."

When Backus proposed the FORTRAN project, IBM quickly approved. He started recruiting the FORTRAN team in 1954, adding people one by one, until there were ten members. It was a young group, all still in their twenties and thirties when FORTRAN was released in 1957. The team was heavy with math training, but their backgrounds were varied—a crystallographer, a cryptographer, a chess wizard, an employee loaned from United Aircraft, a researcher from the Massachusetts Institute of Technology (MIT), a young woman who joined the project straight out of Vassar College. Lois Haibt was that young Vassar graduate, and forty years later she recalled, "They took anyone who seemed to have an aptitude for problem-solving skills—bridge players, chess players, whoever."

They worked together in one open room,

their desks side by side. They often worked at night because that was the only time they could get valuable time on a computer to test and debug the code for their experimental project. The odd hours and the close work bred camaraderie. They were a young, tight-knit group brimming with energy and enthusiasm. They saw themselves as outsiders, trying to do something that had never been done in a brand-new field with few, if any, established rules. "We were the hackers of those days," recalled Richard Goldberg, when he was 76.

To relax, they took afternoon breaks for coffee and donuts at a nearby diner and, in winter, they occasionally fled to Central Park for snowball fights. They also enjoyed lunchtime games of kriegspiel (German for "war game"). Kriegspiel is a form of "blind chess." Two players sit side by side, each with a board, and a divider blocks the view of each other's board. Each player makes moves in turn, and tries to imagine the moves the opponent makes. There is a referee who provides clues—which means announcing moves, when a piece is captured, or when a player cannot make a move because an opponent's piece blocks the way. For a certain kind of mind, kriegspiel was recess.

Making a programming language that was understandable to humans was the easy part of the team's work, though it did require scientists and engineers to learn a series of machine commands and the shorthand abbreviations of the computer language. Still, the real achievement of FORTRAN was what happened underneath—code that took the FORTRAN formulas written by people and automatically generated the ones and zeros of machine code, which the computer understood. Computer time was a precious, costly resource back then. If programs written in FORTRAN had run slowly, consuming a lot of machine time, it never would have been adopted. But FORTRAN made a leap in programming automation that most computer veterans at the time thought was impossible. FORTRAN enabled ordinary scientists and engineers to write programs that ran on a computer as efficiently as the ones so painstakingly crafted by the programming elite.

FORTRAN was a turning point, a tool that widened the horizons of computing. No one would argue that computers were easy to use in those days, but FORTRAN made them far easier to use.

Today, higher-level programming languages are common, but the FORTRAN team was in uncharted territory for three years, and it was difficult, often frustrating, toil. Backus came away from his team's success with an informal theory of innovation—about what it takes—that surely applies to endeavors well beyond computing. "You need the willingness to fail all the time," he explained. "You have to generate many ideas and then you have to work very hard only to discover that they don't work. And you keep doing that over and over until you find one that does work."

From BASIC to Billionaires

FORTRAN helped, but computing was still a luxury. Computers were confined to major universities, government agencies, and large corporations. They were forbidding machines, housed in locked rooms, protected by security guards. It was as if a computer was some sacred object. Only specially trained people could actually touch a computer. Scientists and engineers prepared a program, handed it to a white-coated technician, and typically waited days for the results. Most people saw

Retired Dartmouth math professor Thomas Kurtz with some of the old equipment in the computer room called the "Machine Room" at Dartmouth College in Hanover, New Hampshire, 2004.

computers as giant calculators, even if a handful of visionaries understood the potential reach of computing.

The road to the routine computing of today—where owning and using computers is part of everyday life—came in a series of steps, hardware and software working hand in hand. In the early 1960s, computer time-sharing was a hardware-and-software innovation that opened computing to more and more people—

and helped pave the way for the personal computer.

Time-shared computing really proved itself at Dartmouth College. In a time-shared system, many people used a central computer at once, each typing in their commands from a terminal with a keyboard and sharing the computer. It was called time-sharing because the computer time was expensive and carefully metered. The experiment at Dartmouth was not only a technical achievement, but also a strong signal that computing was recognized as a technology with a broad impact on society. Thomas Kurtz, a young Dartmouth professor, and an older colleague, John Kemeny, clearly understood that computers would be more than just big number-crunching machines. They would be vital tools in managing businesses and running the government. Kurtz and Kemeny believed that a basic appreciation of computing—the power and shortcomings of this versatile technology— was important for all students, not just the science and math whizzes. Computing, the two professors figured, would affect everyone in society, so computing should be taught to all students.

Kurtz and Kemeny created an easy-to-use computer language for students called BASIC, for Beginner's All-purpose Symbolic Instruction Code. And they began to teach programming on the university's time-shared system. Each Dartmouth student got forty-five minutes of computing time a week.

A time-sharing computer could only juggle so many users at once; more than a couple hundred users, and it would crash. Imagine having to wait your turn to get on the Internet. And the time-sharing systems were incredibly slow by today's standards, as students waited up to ten seconds for the Dartmouth computer to respond. Today, a ten-second wait from when you press a key on your keyboard to when a letter appears on the screen is an eternity—a sure sign that your computer is sick.

Yet, sitting at their terminals in the 1960s, the Dartmouth students felt that the machine was alive, responding individually to each student's keyboard commands. In the 1960s and 1970s, time-sharing systems using the BASIC language devised at Dartmouth were how students of all ages around the country got a sense of personal computing.

One of those students would be a thirteen-year-old at a private school in Seattle, Bill Gates. The young man would eventually go on to found Microsoft, help build the personal computer industry, and become one of the richest people in the world. Not that any of that was evident when his father, William H. Gates II, a lawyer, and his mother, Mary, a schoolteacher, decided to send their smart but unruly son to the Lakeside School, starting in seventh grade.

The private boys school had a jacket-and-tie dress code, and a reputation for discipline. His parents figured it might be just the place to straighten young Bill out. "It wasn't as if he was some obvious super-bright kid," his father said later. "I think we recognize it better looking back than we did at the time. At the time, we just thought he was trouble."

The mothers club at the Lakeside School chose to use some of the money from their annual rummage sale to buy a terminal and time on a computer for the students. It was a rather progressive idea in the late 1960s, and a decision for which Bill Gates will always be grateful. The first software program he wrote was for playing tic-tac-toe, and it ran on a computer he described as "huge and cumbersome and slow and absolutely compelling."

Gates and some other Lakeside students (including Paul Allen, who would become cofounder of Microsoft) spent more and more time in the computer room, and their BASIC programs became increasingly sophisticated. "I realized later," Gates said, "that part of the appeal must have been that here was an enormous, expensive, grown-up machine and we, the kids, could control it. We were too young to drive or do any of the other things that adults could have fun at, but we could give this big machine orders and it would always obey."

His observation nicely captures the emotional pull of "personal computing," the sense of human control over an intriguing new technology. It was a bracing experience, and before long the concept of personal computing would change from the illusion provided by time-sharing to the reality of literally owning one's own machine.

A groundbreaking innovation in hardware opened the door to the personal computer revolution, by drastically shrinking the size and price of a computer. It was the invention of the microprocessor, the central computing brain of a personal computer.

By the late 1960s, engineers and entrepreneurs in the California valley south of San Francisco were hard at work trying to figure out the practical uses of packing transistors on silicon wafers. *(On page 125, you can read a* New York Times *article written when the transistor was first invented.)* Transistors were the tiny, sleek next generation of on/off switches, the gatekeepers of power signals flowing through electrical devices. First came the mechanical relay, then the vacuum tube, and then the transistor. Each new generation was a huge improvement. The transistor did everything the vacuum tube could do—switch on or off, and amplify electric current—but did it better. The transistor was smaller, generated less heat, and did not burn out.

Transistors, of course, are used in all kinds of products that use electronics, big and small, from airplanes to wristwatches. But computers—those universal machines—proved to have a limitless appetite for transistors. The more digital switches, handling ones and zeros, the greater the potential for computers to do all kinds of work—rapid calculations or games or simulating weather patterns. And silicon, one of the most common elements in the world, the stuff of sand, was the ideal material for making microscopic transistors, crammed onto a single, thumbnail-sized sliver. The silicon chip that is the central processing brain of a notebook computer today has about 150 million transistors.

So the valley south of San Francisco, once known for its fruit orchards, became known as Silicon Valley.

In 1969, a small company that was only a year old, called Intel, received an order to produce chips for a Japanese maker of desktop electronic calculators. The Japanese company wanted a single-purpose chip designed only for math calculations. But the lead engineer on the project, Ted Hoff, pushed instead for a general-purpose design. Why not open things up to any kind of calculator or device, not just cater to the whim of one customer? It would be more interesting work, Hoff figured, and a smart business move. His bosses at Intel agreed, and the company went on to make a microprocessor in 1971. It was an open, programmable chip. Software could be written to run on the Intel chip, so the chip could do whatever it was programmed to do.

At the time, Intel did not have the computer industry in mind, and the early microprocessors were not very powerful. Yet some people—mostly electronics enthusiasts—soon realized that the microprocessor could be used as the engine of a small, general-purpose computer. Up in Seattle, Bill Gates and Paul Allen read about the Intel invention. "The event that started everything for us business-wise was when I found an article in a 1971 electronics magazine about Intel's 4004 chip, which was the world's first microprocessor," Allen said. "It made me realize that computing was going to be a lot cheaper than it had ever been and that a lot more people would have access to computers."

Gates and Allen had become skilled programmers. They took jobs debugging software for corporations, and even started a short-lived company, Traf-O-Data, which built a computer to count car traffic on highways. The two talked about trying to write a version of BASIC for the first Intel microprocessors. But Gates persuaded Allen to hold off until a faster, more powerful chip arrived. In 1975, they made their move.

By then, both of them were living in the

Boston area. Allen, who is nearly three years older, had dropped out of college and was working for a computer company. Gates, who eventually became an excellent student in high school, was attending Harvard University. Dad needn't have worried about his troublesome son, after all.

The January 1975 issue of *Popular Electronics* magazine announced the first microcomputer kit, the MITS Altair. The powder-blue box was powered by the newest Intel microprocessor, the 8080, and the whole kit cost $400. It was a bare bones offering, but it was a real computer—a reality Gates and Allen instantly grasped. And they rushed off to develop a commercial version of BASIC that would run on the Altair. "Bill and I were anxious to start our own company," Allen recalled. "We realized we had to do it then or we'd forever lose the opportunity to make it in microcomputer software."

MITS was located in Albuquerque, New Mexico, and its president was Ed Roberts, an imposing six-foot-four former air force officer.

Gates and Allen moved quickly to try to get the inside track as the software supplier for the Altair. "So we called this guy Ed Roberts," Gates recalled years later. "We had a fairly aggressive posture. We said, 'We have a BASIC. Do you want it?'"

When they called, Gates and Allen were bluffing. They had no software. Roberts was skeptical, and told them what he had told others making similar offers. He would buy the first BASIC that he actually saw running on an Altair. And he would be an eager buyer, since the Altair badly needed a working programming language.

The Altair came with a front panel of lights and switches. To communicate with the machine, the first hardy Altair users had to load information into the computer one bit at a time, by flipping the front-panel switches. After processing the information and instructions, the Altair would spit out its answer as a pattern of lights flashing on the front panel. The switches-and-lights routine was reminiscent of the way the pioneer programmers of the 1950s worked on the massive computers of their day. The Altair wasn't going far if that was how people had to program the machine.

In early 1975, MITS had just begun shipping Altair kits, and they were scarce. Gates and Allen could not wait to get their hands on one, so they improvised. Allen wrote a program that mimicked the Intel microprocessor that powered the Altair—a software simulation of the Altair. They loaded that virtual Altair program on a huge computer at Harvard's computer center. That is where Gates wrote most of the code for their original BASIC for the Altair.

Eventually, questions were raised about Gates's marathon use of the university computer center to start a business. Gates could have been expelled, but in the end no

The first personal computer, the Altair, was released in 1975. Data was entered by flipping switches on its front panel, and responses were communicated through flashing lights on the same panel.

action was taken. Years later, Gates would contribute millions of dollars to Harvard, more than making amends, it seems, for bending the rules.

The BASIC that Gates wrote for the Altair packed a lot into a very small space. It was fast, and it had an impressive set of features for a language that initially ran in a memory space for only 4K, or 4,000 bytes of data (standard personal computers in 2009 came with at least 2 billion bytes of memory, or 500,000 times as much). Nearly thirty years later, Gates still savored his achievement back in the Harvard computer center. "Actually, making a BASIC run in that little memory is a real feat," he recalled. "Of all the programming I've done, it's the thing I'm most proud of."

Gates and Allen chose BASIC, without hesitation, as their programming language because it was familiar to young electronics fanatics, the most promising market for the Altair. When they had programmed in school, it was in BASIC. Time-shared computers became obsolete, but BASIC made the transition to the personal computer era. BASIC was also an "open" technology. Dartmouth put no real restrictions on its use. It was free, and it could be tweaked and changed to suit new machines, like the little Altair.

Gates and Allen used BASIC, added their own innovations, and developed the version of the language they sold to MITS. In the contract, they referred to their new company as *Micro-Soft*. The name came from combining the first half of the words "microcomputer" and "software."

Over the years, Microsoft has often been portrayed as a corporate bully. And, in fact, a federal court ruled in 2000 that Microsoft had violated the nation's antitrust laws by abusing its market power to stifle competition, a suit the company later settled with the government. But Microsoft attained its powerful position mainly because it saw that software was something distinct from hardware—that software would have its own life, not only as a technology but also as a market.

Microsoft's success owes a lot to the vision, intelligence, and persistence of Bill Gates. (Paul

Allen, his partner, left Microsoft in 1983 after he was diagnosed with Hodgkin's disease, though he later recovered.) As a skinny young man with big glasses, Gates seemed cast for the part of a computer nerd. It was an easy stereotype, and he was tagged with it starting as a teenager. Gates recalled that when he got the lead role in a play at Lakeside School, "some kids were heard muttering, 'Why did they pick the computer guy?' That's the way I still sometimes get labeled."

Yet Gates is far more than a computer geek. He certainly grasped the bits and bytes of computing, but most of all he saw the opportunity for software that was being opened by the microprocessor and low-cost computing in a way no one else did.

In September 2001, there was a big gathering in Silicon Valley to celebrate the twentieth anniversary of the introduction of the IBM PC. In 1981, IBM's entry into the personal computer business was a watershed, a signal by the industry giant that the personal computer had

Bill Gates, Chairman of Microsoft Corporation, and Paul Allen, now owner of the Portland Trail Blazers, chat during a basketball game in Seattle, March 11, 2003.

arrived. It was no longer a hobbyist's toy. So twenty years later, the industry's leaders came to reminisce and marvel at how much progress they had made since the early days.

I decided to go instead to Cochran, Georgia, where Ed Roberts was a family physician in the rural South. It was a long way from Silicon Valley, and from Albuquerque in the 1970s, when Paul Allen and Bill Gates showed up with Microsoft BASIC. Few people have heard of him, perhaps, but Roberts had his moment in computing history. Over the years, people have credited others with inventing the personal computer, including the Xerox Palo Alto Research Center, Apple Computer, and IBM. Yet Paul Ceruzzi, a technology historian at the Smithsonian Institution, concluded that "H. Edward Roberts, the Altair's designer, deserves credit as the inventor of the personal computer." Other places have their claims. "But Albuquerque it was," Ceruzzi said, "for it was only at MITS that the technical and social components of personal computing converged."

Sitting in his office, where an Altair rested on a corner shelf, Roberts viewed his role in the personal computer revolution with candor and a sense of humor. "Let's not kid anybody," he said. "We were there at the right time, when things fell into place and we were there to put them together."

Roberts sold MITS in 1977 to another now-forgotten microcomputer maker. He agreed not to design computers for five years, and walked away a millionaire. He first bought some farmland in Georgia and then decided to revive a high school dream of becoming a physician. In fact, his introduction to electronics was as a teenager working in a hospital in Miami. The physicians were doing experimental heart surgery, and he built a basic relay computer for a heart-lung machine. "We used a lot of electronics, and that's how I got into it," he explained.

Roberts attended Oklahoma State University in the 1960s. He majored in electrical engineering and spent a lot of time programming engineering problems in FORTRAN on a big IBM machine in the university's computer center. The power of computing "opened up a whole new world," Roberts said. "And I began thinking, 'What if you gave everyone a computer?'"

It would be years before advances in computer hardware and software would begin to bring that goal within reach. But the MITS Altair was a step toward Ed Roberts's belief that "if you give people computers, some amazing things are going to happen."

"It proved to be true," he observed.

4

Icons and iPods

Andy Hertzfeld was a bright teenager and, like a lot of teenagers, he saw rules as things to be tested, if not broken. In 1970, his high school in suburban Philadelphia offered a computer-programming course, and he found he really enjoyed it—the puzzle-solving fun of putting programs together and watching them run to perform calculations or play games. His programming, mostly in BASIC, was done on a keyboard terminal in a classroom, which was

Andy Hertzfeld (center) in 2000.

linked over a telephone line to a machine he never saw, a big time-sharing computer far away.

Hertzfeld's school paid for the computer time by the minute. The school wasn't watching the bills too closely at first. Students were simply cautioned to limit their time on the machine. But Hertzfeld wasn't much listening. He was having too much fun. Soon, he was single-handedly racking up bills at an alarming rate. People took notice after Hertzfeld embarked on a project for the school. He wrote a program for matching partners for the junior prom. He handed out questionnaires that asked students to answer simple questions about themselves, their preferences and interests. Hundreds of boys and girls participated, mostly out of curiosity. Who will the computer pick for me? Will it be someone I like or know or someone I've never considered dating?

Hertzfeld collected the questionnaires, assembled the data and ran his program. When the long-awaited list came back, he was stunned. The computer matched one girl with a third of the boys in the class. To Hertzfeld, it seemed obvious that one girl could not go out with thirty, fifty, or a hundred boys at a time. Yet the dating blunder was not obvious to the computer, unschooled in human ways—which is to say not programmed to eliminate multiple matches.

The "prom bug" was not only an embarrassment to Hertzfeld, but the episode also called attention to how much time he was spending on the computer, and to the mounting bills to the school. "I was banned from using the machine," he recalled.

Still, it was only a temporary setback. Hertzfeld wormed his way back into the computer center by proving to the school administrators that he could write useful programs, like one that calculated the grade point average and class rank for each student. But the prom bug had taught Hertzfeld an important and lasting lesson about the inflexible, literal-minded nature of computers.

Years later, Hertzfeld was a member of the team that created the hardware and software of the Apple Macintosh, the computer that really set the pattern for how we interact with computers today. The Macintosh, introduced in 1984, opened the door for millions of ordinary people to use personal computers without a lot of special training. Research projects came before, and Microsoft would follow with Windows. But it was the Macintosh that brought a different look and feel to everyday computing—a more friendly face.

Today, it seems so natural to nudge a computer mouse around to steer a virtual pointer across the computer screen—or navigate with a fingertip across a cell phone touch screen—and to click on icons to do things like open a Web browser, an e-mail program, or a document. The routine is so familiar we don't give it a second thought. But before the Macintosh, most people had not seen a computer mouse. When you turned on a personal computer, you typically saw a black screen with what was called the *command line* at the top, starting with the characters C:\>. It awaited your commands, and the rest was up to you.

Starting a program or opening a document required some knowledge of the interior architecture of the computer—its directory and file system—and typing in commands, in a shorthand text that had to be memorized. To see the directory of files, for example, you would type *dir* in the command line and then hit the Enter key. It felt too much like programming for many people.

The Macintosh, instead, presented itself

more visually, using what is known as a *graphical user interface*—the icons on the screen, which can be opened simply with a mouse click. And the Macintosh did it at a price that seemed remarkably affordable, $2,500.

The ideas behind the Macintosh stretched back for decades. Those ideas came from scientists who strongly believed that computers were indeed, in Alan Turing's phrase, universal machines—powerful tools that could do all kinds of things. They wanted, even in those days before the personal computer, to make computing a more personal experience accessible to more and more people.

J. C. R. Licklider, a Harvard-trained psychologist, was a founding father of the movement to make computers easier to use. He arrived at the Massachusetts Institute of Technology in 1950 to set up a program to encourage electrical engineers to design with human beings in mind. Licklider had worked on air-defense systems that combined radar and early computers to scan the skies for enemy fighter planes and missiles. In such systems, rapid and clear presentation of information was essential, and Licklider helped design the display consoles. Building the equipment was one thing, but the other challenge was "making a good interface with the user," observed Licklider.

In a 1960 paper, Licklider noted the progress of higher-level computer programming languages like FORTRAN. He said they were a good first step, but still way too complicated. His vision of computers was that they should be automated human assistants—something that would be far easier for humans to communicate with and order to do things. To reach that goal, Licklider added, it would "be necessary to make use of an additional and rather different principle of communication and control."

A groundbreaking demonstration of a new kind of human-computer communication came in 1968 in San Francisco. The event's impresario was Douglas C. Engelbart, a scientist at the Stanford Research Institute, whose work was championed by Licklider and supported with government funds. In the pictures and video of the event, Engelbart, wearing a necktie and white shirt, is a handsome, even-featured man with graying hair, who looks like a television newscaster. But it was the technology that Engelbart and his team showed off that day that made the lasting impression. It was a computer workstation, and images that appeared on a computer desktop were also projected on a twenty-foot screen.

Engelbart used a computer mouse to open up programs and documents. He had invented the computer mouse a few years earlier, after lengthy experiments with other devices that might work alongside a keyboard. Among discarded devices were foot pedals, much like those used on old sewing machines.

In his demonstration, Engelbart split the screen in separate "windows" and showed off documents that held both text and graphics, which could be moved around and edited. Besides the mouse, this was the other big step— being able to present multiple views on the

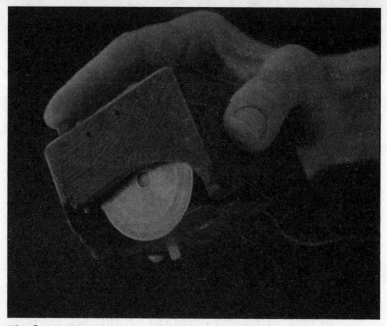

The first computer mouse was housed in a wood case, and tracked movement through two wheels positioned on the horizontal and vertical axes.

screen, as side-by-side windows. The window, Engelbart explained, need not be a flat page of information. The computer window is a lens providing one view of a landscape of digital data—it could be words or pictures, and later music or video. This digital landscape would become known as cyberspace.

When Engelbart finished, the audience gave him a standing ovation. The computer workstation he used was big, clunky, and slow by our standards today. Yet that demonstration in 1968 was historic (some of the equipment he used now resides at the Smithsonian Museum of American History in Washington, D.C.). The technology he presented was a long way from being affordable, however. In 1968, the cost of his screen display alone would have been about $25,000, the equivalent of nearly $140,000 now, adjusted for inflation. This kind of computing was still a very expensive science experiment.

But Engelbart's ideas spread and flourished. Alan Kay, then a young computer scientist, recalled the 1968 demonstration in San Francisco as "one of the greatest experiences of my life." Kay would go on to be a leader of Xerox Palo Alto Research Center, or Xerox PARC. The copier company set up the research group in Silicon Valley in the 1970s, and its mission was to search for the "Office of the Future."

Building on the work of Engelbart and others,

the Xerox research team developed the modern metaphor of computing—the computer screen as a desktop. The basic ingredients are those familiar to us today—a desktop arrayed with little pictures known as icons, overlapping windows, and simplifying "menus" with choices that drop down, with a mouse click, from words at the top of the screen, like File, Edit, and Tools. These drop-down menus are intended to make it easier for you to find the many functions and

Steven P. Jobs, left, chairman of Apple Computer, Inc., and John Sculley, president, introduce the new Macintosh personal computer in 1984.

features on the computer. At Xerox PARC, the desktop concept was realized in a prototype machine called the Alto.

Xerox never successfully brought its impressive technology to market. That would happen at Apple years after a few memorable visits to Xerox PARC, by Steve Jobs, Apple's cofounder, and others. The Apple team certainly got ideas, and inspiration, from the Xerox lab. But it took years of work and innovation to translate the ideas into a workable, affordable, friendly computer with the graphical user interface that we now take for granted. And Apple did it.

In the 1970s and 1980s, Apple had an aura of counterculture chic. Its logo—a rainbow-striped apple with a bite taken out—was a symbol of knowledge and desire, sampled. It was a reference to the biblical story of Eve in the Garden of Eden, tempted by the apple. The Apple logo was playful and maybe a little naughty. One cofounder, Steve Jobs, was a charismatic young man who portrayed Apple less as a company than as a cause. Apple, Jobs insisted, was not making computers; it was making history. The other cofounder, Stephen Wozniak, was an engineering genius with a playful streak, fond of practical jokes.

Apple hired people from different backgrounds with a wider range of skills than other computer companies, and did so by design. The Macintosh, according to Jobs, turned out so well because the people working on it were schooled in music, art, poetry, and medicine, as well as computer science. So it's not surprising that Apple was the company that made computers easier to use. User interface designers determine the face that the computer presents on the screen, and their judgments are as much about design and taste as engineering. What is the visual presentation that is most instinctively understandable, and pleasing, to the people who will use the computer?

Even the Macintosh team's technical experts, like Hertzfeld, a software whiz, had that sensibility. "It's really fun to be in the middle of the technical, precise, and objective computer, and the fuzzy, emotional, subjective human being," Hertzfeld explained. "I've always loved art, especially literature and music, and I think the human element is what can elevate engineering to the realm of art."

Jobs led the Macintosh team. He was not an engineer. He did not build Apple hardware or software himself. But he had been a hands-on student of technology since he was a child, and he possessed an innate sense of design. His greatest talent was in picking and leading product teams. He was much like a difficult and demanding sports coach or orchestra conductor, who inspired and cajoled people to go further and achieve more than they thought they could.

Jobs himself describes his role in those terms. Some people, he says, enjoy pursuits that a single person can accomplish—the "Michelangelo path." Others prefer to seek achievements that are more like a "symphony," he says, a creation beyond the abilities of an individual.

Steve Jobs holds up the Mac-Book Air during his keynote at the 2008 MacWorld Conference in San Francisco.

"Everything I've done is like that—a team sport," Jobs explained several years ago, talking in his kitchen in Palo Alto, California. "I think I have taste in choosing good people, and taste in products."

Jobs grew up in Silicon Valley in the 1960s and 1970s. Adopted as a baby, Jobs was reared in a blue-collar household in Los Altos by Paul Jobs, a machinist for a company that made lasers, and Clara, an accountant. Jobs began tinkering with electronics even before he reached his teens. That was not unusual in Silicon Valley at the time, but few were as enterprising. As a twelve-year-old, when Jobs was short of parts for a project, he simply picked up the phone and called the largest electronics company in Silicon Valley, Hewlett-Packard. And he went to the top, asking to speak to William Hewlett, the cofounder, who took the call from a kid named Jobs whom he had never heard of. Hewlett was a bit taken aback, but the young man proved convincing. Jobs got his parts.

Soon, Jobs had started a brisk little business in electronic gear in high school. He would buy old stereos, fix them, and sell them at a profit. Steve Jobs and Steve Wozniak met because of their shared passion for electronics, and the two struck up a lasting friendship, even though Wozniak was five years older.

In 1972, when he graduated from high school in Silicon Valley, Jobs recalled, "the very strong scent of the 1960s was still there." The 1960s counterculture was about personal freedom, following your instincts, experimenting with sex and drugs. It was definitely not about settling down, getting married, and working for a big company. There was a certain rootless romance to it all.

After high school, Jobs attended Reed College. He dropped out of school after six months, but stayed in Portland, Oregon, for another eighteen months studying Eastern religions, becoming vegetarian, and dropping into college classes that interested him. He then returned home to Silicon Valley, and took a job at Atari, a video-game maker. He worked long enough to earn money for a trip to India. After a few months, Jobs came back to California, and soon reconnected with his friend Wozniak. They founded Apple in 1976, starting small in the Jobs family garage. Jobs was twenty years old.

Jobs speaks of Apple products in the language of emotion. The Macintosh, Jobs reflected in his Palo Alto home, was "the first adult love of my life." Later, he added, "At its core, the Mac represented a spirit and a point of view, a love of computing and a desire to bring it to everyone." The notion of taste is important to him. Great products, he says, are a triumph of taste, of "trying to expose yourself to the best things humans have done and then trying to bring those things into what you are doing."

The design choices in the Macintosh were made with an eye toward easing the frustrations of using computers. The thought process itself is instructive. One of the big debates in the user-interface field has been over the number of buttons on a mouse, a debate that continues. At Xerox PARC, the Alto had three buttons, like Douglas Engelbart's original mouse at the Stanford Research Institute. Microsoft later adopted a two-button mouse for personal computers running Windows. *(The computer mouse began to be widely marketed in the early 1980s. A* New York Times *article about the new mouse craze can be found on page 137.)*

Apple opted for a one-button mouse. Not everyone liked the one-button mouse, but there was a user philosophy behind Apple's choice. Guy Tribble, a member of the original Macintosh team, explained the philosophy with a recollection. Tribble, a software engineer and a physician, was studying to be a neurologist at the University of Washington when he joined Apple and, while at Apple, went back to school to finish his degree. He remembered being in Seattle, going by a video-game parlor and watching some nine-year-olds play fairly sophisticated warfare and strategy games like "Space Invaders." They learned to play not by reading instructions, but by watching an experienced player for a game or two.

It left an impression. "The point was you could watch someone do it and then you could do it yourself," Tribble said, adding that the same approach was used in designing the Macintosh. "It was really optimized for ease of learning—ease of use is probably a misnomer. And it's a lot like teaching a new procedure in medical school—see one, do one, teach one. For very visual things, that works. And the Mac was a visual thing."

The Macintosh, as it turned out, was not an instant success. The new machine was elegant and easy to use, but it was a couple of years before other companies made enough software applications to make it a really useful tool. In

1985, a year after the Macintosh was introduced, Steve Jobs was pushed out of the company. But he was brought back in 1997 and, under him, Apple brought out a flurry of innovative products including the iPod.

The Apple iPod has extended computing to digital media. Apple's hardware and software became how millions of people began using a stylish, handheld computer to browse through and play their libraries of music, often thousands of songs. Before, music collections meant tall stacks of CDs. Digital music players could hold thousands of music tracks in a device smaller than a paperback book.

When the iPod was introduced in 2001, it was not the first digital music player. Other models could hold more songs, and most of them were less expensive than the iPod, which was priced at $399. Early skeptics sneered that the iPod was an acronym for "Idiots Price Our Devices." But they were proved wrong. No one else could match the digital music experience that Apple delivered. The iPod won because it was easy, even fun, to use. Its hardware and software was a triumph of user interface design. You didn't need an owner's manual to figure out how to organize, find, and play music. And you could navigate through all the stored songs by grazing a finger over the center wheel. People loved their iPods. The iPod became the winner in the digital music player market. Apple won even though companies like Sony and Philips had far more experience with music-playing gear and offerings from Rio and Zen were less costly. None of them could match Apple's software skills, though. Later iPod models also played television shows and music videos.

To Steve Jobs, the success of the iPod—and, six years after, the iPhone—was a vindication of the Apple philosophy. "As technology becomes more complex," he observed, "Apple's core strength of knowing how to make very sophisticated technology comprehensible to mere mortals is in even greater demand."

Someday, the iPod may lose its lead and be overtaken by competing products. Yet whatever happens, the iPod was a pioneering product that showed the way. Small, light, and easy to use, the iPod was a media computer for everyone. It brought the power of computing into the daily lives of millions of people with hardware and software that didn't feel like a computer. And that is certain to be one important direction in the future as computing increasingly gives us the power to store and retrieve amazing amounts of digital information—whether a song on a music player in your hand or the answer to some mystery of science in a research document somewhere on the World Wide Web.

"Some Amazing Things Are Going to Happen"

The World Wide Web is a vast storehouse of information—a digital library on the Internet, accessible to people all over the world. And the Web is a new tool for an old problem.

Information is the raw material of knowledge and progress. Get the right pieces of information, put them together in just the right way, and ideas and inventions spring to life. But how best to gather, store, and find useful stuff?

It has been a vexing challenge at least since the third century B.C., when Ptolemy I of Egypt began building the Great Library of Alexandria. The grand building was to be a universal library that would hold every book on every imaginable subject. King Ptolemy wrote to all the leaders of the known world to ask for a copy of every book by every author. A royal decree ordered that any book brought into the city of Alexandria would be confiscated and copied.

The king's librarians figured they would have to collect about 500,000 scrolls if the library were to have all the world's books. Today, the Library of Congress receives that many printed items each year. But even in ancient Egypt, the librarians soon realized that the flood of scrolls coming into Alexandria would overwhelm any reader. So they chose the works they deemed most important, wrote brief descriptions, and listed them in catalogs. The catalogs were among the earliest recommended reading lists or, in Internet terms, search results.

Over the centuries, new technologies—

from the printing press to computer networks—made it easier to create and distribute information. New knowledge, new science, and mass education meant more people were generating and consuming information. The scientific advances of the first half of the twentieth century added enormously to the information overload. In 1945, as World War II was nearing its end, Vannevar Bush, the head of the agency that coordinated scientific research for the war effort, made a provocative recommendation.

In an article in *The Atlantic Monthly* magazine of July 1945, titled "As We May Think," Bush suggested that a new frontier for science should be to make the world's bewildering accumulation of knowledge more accessible and more useful. The time had come, Bush declared, for technology to focus on extending the powers of the mind instead of the wartime goals of extending man's physical powers of speed, force, and destruction. Bush noted the "growing mountain of research" in the sciences and other disciplines. To solve the problem, he proposed a "Memex," a mechanized desk with a screen and a keyboard. He envisioned a machine that would store all of a person's books, records, magazines, and communications on microfilm, using instant photography. The information in the Memex could be searched and retrieved by tapping out simple codes on the keyboard. Storage, in Bush's vision, would be virtually unlimited. "If the user inserted five thousand pages of material a day," he wrote, "it would take him hundreds of years to fill the repository."

The Memex was a dream machine, but an influential one. It would get people thinking for years to come. As a desklike machine for personal use, the Memex anticipated the personal computer. And Bush's vision of a limitless storehouse of information at one's fingertips pointed toward the Internet and the Web.

As it turned out, it was the fear of nuclear attack that helped bring the realization of Bush's dream. At the height of the Cold War, when the United States and the Soviet Union were rival superpowers, each side feared that the other might unleash its arsenal of nuclear missiles. (Neither side was foolish enough to try, and risk annihilation in a counterattack, so it never became a real war—but a standoff in a "cold war" instead.) But to prepare for the worst, the United States Department of Defense funded a research project to build a communications network that could survive a nuclear attack. So in the 1960s and 1970s, a group of scientists in the United States built the beginnings of the Internet. It was a research network, connecting university and government laboratories. It was decentralized by design, so that if one or a few computers on the network failed (blown up, presumably), the people in the other computer labs could still communicate with each other. Their e-mail and other information would be automatically rerouted to take another path to their destination. That way, the network could survive a nuclear strike, even if some of the computer equivalents of power plants or relay stations were knocked out.

The Internet was at first merely a research project. A few hundred researchers used it to share information and communicate. It was a small community of people who tended to have similar backgrounds and values. Its technology and its culture were open and friendly, as if a neighborhood in a small town. People trusted their neighbors.

The decentralized design of the Internet also made it easy to keep adding more computers, like an endless spider web, with no center, that just kept growing. But the growth came very slowly at first, and only really took off in the 1990s. First, at least three things had to happen. By the 1990s, millions of people had personal computers. Personal computers had to be seen as tools of communication and not just calculation. E-mail gave people a taste of the communication potential of computers linked to a network, as people sent typed messages to each other. But what really helped was when computers could communicate with each other, so information of all kinds, stored on computers anywhere, could be found and shared.

What that leap made possible—and made the Internet a mass medium used by everyone—was the World Wide Web. The Web, for short, is the technology for presenting, identifying, and linking documents over the Internet. And those Web pages can hold all kinds of media including text, images, animations, video, and sound. The terms *Internet* and *Web* tend to be used interchangeably, and they are closely related. Put simply, the Internet network is the digital "pipe" while the Web we see and hear is made up of the stuff that flows through the pipe. And everything that travels over the Internet is digitized information—that is, all of it can be reduced to the ones and zeros of computer code.

The Web, like most advances in computing, was enthusiastically embraced and commercially exploited first in the United States. Yet the Web was not the work of a computer scientist at a leading American university or company. It was the creation of a British physicist, working in the shadow of the Swiss Alps, at Europe's CERN (European Organization for Nuclear Research) physics laboratory outside Geneva, Tim Berners-Lee.

As a computer whiz, Berners-Lee may have had a genetic advantage. He is the son of two English mathematicians, Conway Berners-Lee and Mary Lee Woods, who worked on the team that programmed an early computer, the Ferranti Mark I in 1951. And he grew up in a household where computers were discussed. One evening when Berners-Lee was a teenager, he recalled a conversation at home. His father was reading about the brain, looking for ideas on how computers might be made intuitive, able to make connections as humans do. The father and son discussed the subject briefly. "But the idea stayed with me," Berners-Lee observed, "that computers could become much more powerful if they could be programmed to link otherwise unconnected information."

In 1976, Berners-Lee graduated from Oxford University with a degree in physics, but he was an engineer by instinct. Fascinated by computing and the potential of low-cost microprocessors, he built his own personal computer, using an old television for a monitor. He became a software designer, and over the next several years he had a series of jobs at big companies and small ones.

Throughout those years, Berners-Lee continued to think about how to use computers to organize information more efficiently. He even wrote a program for himself for storing personal information that he called *Enquire*, which had some linking features, a start toward his later work on Web technology.

Berners-Lee joined the European physics lab, outside Geneva, in 1984 as a technical worker. His job was to design software that would help the scientists by making it easier for them to use and share documents and databases. But he was thinking well beyond the physics lab and reading anything that related to his interests. That research took him back to read Vannevar Bush's article in *The Atlantic Monthly*, review the research of Douglas Engelbart, and also the ideas of Ted Nelson, who coined the term *hypertext* in the mid-1960s. Computers, Nelson predicted, would be "literary machines" that enabled people to publish in a new format—hypertext—so a reader could follow links to related documents or other books.

By the mid-1980s, Berners-Lee was taking note of the Internet. He was impressed and he

Tim Berners-Lee, the man who invented the Internet's World Wide Web, poses in his Massachusetts Institute of Technology office, October 2, 1995, in Cambridge, Massachusetts.

saw an opportunity to apply what he learned about linking documents and information.

The Web can be seen as a marriage of the Internet and hypertext. To join them, Berners-Lee created the software for presenting, addressing, and transferring multimedia documents over the Internet. Every time you go onto the Web, and browse around, you see Berners-Lee's handiwork, even if you don't know it.

All Web pages contain computer code, called hypertext mark-up language, or HTML. It wraps around the text and pictures, and tells the computer, "This is a picture, it should go here. This is text, it should go there." Every Web page has an address, like www.google.com, so a computer can find it. The technical term for such an address is a uniform resource locator, or URL, which Berners-Lee also created.

When you move your computer cursor over text or an image on a Web page, and your cursor changes shape to look like a hand with the index finger pointed up, that signifies a hypertext link to another Web page. You click to see that page, hear the music, or see the video. The set of software rules for sending multimedia files over the Internet is the hypertext transfer protocol. And this digital handshake between two computers, known as HTTP, is another Berners-Lee invention.

By the end of 1990, Berners-Lee had written the basic software that was the foundation of the Web, and he released it over the Internet. The Web built slowly at first, but then gathered speed. Scientists and students led the way, but soon its popularity snowballed as more people tried it and told their friends about it. Software companies designed programs to make it easier to browse the Web and to build Web pages.

The Web became a phenomenon, a cultural force, and a huge market as companies saw the potential to suddenly reach customers worldwide over the Web. Web-based companies trying to sell everything from diesel engines to dog food online sprung up at a furious pace by the late 1990s. The center of the boom was in Silicon Valley.

I first met Berners-Lee in 1995, as the money mania surrounding the Internet was just getting underway. The first handful of Internet millionaires had been minted in Silicon Valley. By then, Berners-Lee had left the European physics lab and moved to the Massachusetts Institute of Technology. MIT had become the home of the World Wide Web Consortium, which helps govern the Web, and Berners-Lee was its director.

People were making fortunes on Web businesses, and many more would, but Berners-Lee was not one of them. In the early 1990s, he said, he often thought of how he might get rich. In the end, however, working independently to keep the Web open and outside the influence of any one company seemed like the right thing to do. "I wanted to see the Web proliferate, not sink my life's hours into worrying over a product release," he explained.

His appearance and manner suggested someone more interested in chasing ideas than money. A slender man with an unruly head of thinning blond hair, Berners-Lee had a reputation for speaking as he thinks, rapidly. To try to slow him down, colleagues at the European physics lab used to urge him to speak in French rather than English. It helped only slightly.

His sense of humor was offbeat. Asked about his favorite Web sites, Berners-Lee mentioned sites put up by people pursuing the fastest way to light a barbeque. One showed a person using three gallons of liquid nitrogen to get forty pounds of charcoal burning in three seconds. It must have violated innumerable health and safety laws. "It's seriously stupid behavior," Berners-Lee said, grinning gleefully.

The Internet and the Web, like all technologies, are tools. How they are used depends on who is using them. Today, we can find almost anything over the Internet—music, movies, goods to buy, and information on every imaginable subject. We can browse around and send messages anywhere in the world instantly and without cost. Yet that same power and reach also makes us more easily accessible to strangers, intruders, and con artists.

The Web's creator is an optimist. He is betting on the power of information, and the good it can bring, to far outweigh the bad. The Web, Berners-Lee explained, means more people around the world have more information, and eventually that should mean more innovation and creativity in all kinds of fields. The creative process, in his view, involves placing a good mind in an environment rich in information—a "Web of information," he calls it. "Creativity is a Web-like process, it's nonlinear but not random, either," Berners-Lee said. "It requires ideas just floating—that is the state in which the mind can jiggle them into an insight."

The Web is part of everyday life, but its creator is scarcely a household name. "Tim Berners-Lee is the unsung hero of the Internet," observed Eric Schmidt, a computer scientist, who became Google's CEO. "If this were a traditional science, Berners-Lee would win a Nobel Prize. What he's done is that significant."

Berners-Lee designed imaginative tools that others could use and build on. And Google would become one of the more significant enterprises built on the Web. The popular Internet search engine was the brainchild of two graduate students at Stanford University, Larry Page and Sergey Brin. The Google corporate mission, it states, is "to organize the world's information and make it universally accessible and useful," an Internet-age echo of the ambition of the Library of Alexandria.

Google was an early innovator—and market leader—in search technology, a field that seems a promising path toward artificial intelligence. Yet there are other paths as well. Companies like Microsoft and IBM, startups in Silicon Valley, and researchers at leading universities are all pursuing the long-held dream of programming a computer to mimic human intelligence. And there are many different ways to try to make computers "smarter."

One ambitious goal that scientists are pursuing is to program computers to decipher the meaning and nuance of human language. In computer science, this is called *natural-language processing*. Natural language means how people write or speak, as opposed to computer languages. No computing programs are yet really good at natural-language inquiries—which would be just asking questions, written or spoken. The ideal would be to have a conversation with the computer to learn more about some subject—rock stars, sports teams, or homework. But today, the best we can do is type in a few key words. Then the search-engine software crawls the Web, identifying and sorting results likely to be relevant to our inquiry.

Yet scientists in companies and universities around the world are working on the artificial intelligence challenge of enabling computers to understand questions, supply answers, and learn as humans do. It would represent the highest level of man–machine communication—we could talk to the machine, literally.

And it would represent the realization of the vision that Alan Turing had so many years ago of a computer that could be programmed to simulate human intelligence—a truly universal machine. *(You can read more about the future of A.I. on page 141.)*

The talking-and-learning computer is a long way off, if it comes at all, but it is one direction where computing is headed. What else? We can't say for sure, but it's a safe bet that computers will continue to get smaller and smarter. And that means they will find more and more ways to play a role in our lives, become easier to use and carry around, and be folded into more products as if invisible.

To shrink the personal computer further, researchers are now working on the computer-on-a-card. The card itself would be about the size of a credit card. It would hold all your personal information, contacts, e-mail, school reports, music, and so on, and be a real computer with a microprocessor and storage. The card could be slipped into devices large or small, and its clever software would figure out what information you wanted and how to display it. Slip the card into a slot on a flat-screen monitor, and it becomes a desktop personal computer. Slip the card into a handheld media player, and it shows you your music and videos. Slip it into a cell phone handset, and it becomes the ultimate smart phone.

Sensors will increasingly be everywhere. Sensors are not full-fledged computers, but they can collect, store, and send information, including about their own location and movement. Computers can then process that information to instruct machines. One possible use is to make smart cars that know their location on the road, the location of other cars, and speed of travel. These smart cars will be able to automatically avoid collisions, reducing highway accidents and traffic deaths. In recent years, the Pentagon has sponsored an annual contest that attracts the nation's leading university researchers to bring their robotic vehicles to the California desert, to navigate a 132-mile course. They have made great progress. Some of the robot vehicles can finish the course, but none yet approach the speed, quick reactions, or maneuverability of a car with a person at the wheel.

Today, the home robot is merely a machine that can handle simple vacuuming. But advancing technology holds the promise of a robot that is more like a tireless, automated cleaning person. There may be tiny sensors in your clothes, shoes, sheets, blankets, books, stuffed animals, tennis racquets, soccer balls, or whatever is in your room. The robot could store an image of a cleaned-up room—everything in its place— and the sensors store information like whether a shirt on the floor has been worn. On command, the robot will clean up the room. *(Turn to page 146 for more potential uses of computers in future daily life.)*

Progress in computing and genetics will open the way to making the practice of medicine increasingly personalized and predictive. A reading of your genes and simulations of your body's metabolism will mean that drugs and therapies can be tailored to you. No more standard doses of prescription drugs, and they will be more effective, with lower risk of unhealthy side effects. In the future, tiny implants will be able to monitor the effects on your body of what you eat, your exercise, and sleeping habits. You may be sent messages, "Okay, that was your third cheeseburger this week. To offset the calories and fat intake, and bring down your cholesterol, you have to increase your exercise to the equivalent of a seven-mile run."

Computers have the potential to nag more persistently and perhaps more irritatingly than any parent ever could. But there is also enormous promise to use computing to improve health care. Some researchers predict that within twenty years or so, computing, nanotechnology, and genetics may make it possible to prevent the onset of killer diseases and even halt the aging process. They say that nanobots—microscopic machines—will be dispatched painlessly throughout the body to clean out arteries, repair damaged cells, and flush out toxins. The idea is that we will be able to literally program our bodies, almost as if programming a computer, to stop the degeneration of cells, which has always been regarded as an inescapable fact of aging. So, in theory, people who are teenagers today could live forever.

Impossible? Perhaps, but the technology itself leads people to think of limitless horizons. Computers are so malleable, and can be used for so many things. The only sure thing is that the computing revolution is just getting under-way, and where it goes will be determined not by machines but by human innovation and imagination.

Just where that leads is hard to say. When he was creating the tools for the World Wide Web, Tim Berners-Lee could not predict that people would build billions of Web pages. The Apple Macintosh team could not know they were setting the pattern for how people would use personal computers for decades. Bill Gates could not conceive of all the things that people would do with personal computers, or what a huge business software would become. John Backus did not know that FORTRAN would be the lasting model for higher-level programming languages. And the artists and computer scientists at Pixar could not foresee how successful their collaboration would be.

Yet they all stand as proof that Ed Roberts, the father of the personal computer, was right: "If you give bright people computers, some amazing things are going to happen."

Timeline

Early ninth century The *algorithm*, a basic principle in math and computing, first comes into use about 1,200 years ago. It is named for Persian mathematician, al-Khāwrizmī.

1834–35 Charles Babbage, an English mathematician, draws up elaborate plans for his Analytical Engine, a conceptual forerunner of the modern computer.

1936 British mathematician Alan Turing introduces the idea of a "universal machine" that can simulate any calculating device, even the human brain.

1939 Stanford engineers William Hewlett and David Packard start Hewlett-Packard in a garage in Palo Alto, California, beginning a tradition of garage entrepreneurs in Silicon Valley.

1946 ENIAC, short for Electronic Numerical Integrator and Computer, is demonstrated. It is considered to be the first electronic digital computer.

1947 The transistor, the fundamental building block of electronic devices, is developed by researchers at Bell Labs.

1948 IBM's Selective Sequence Electronic Calculator, a room-sized machine used for scientific calculations, is put on public display in New York City.

1952 On television, a UNIVAC I computer predicts the outcome of the presidential election.

1956 Storing data on magnetic hard disks, allowing faster access to information, begins with IBM's 305 RAMAC.

A conference on the potential of computer-based "artificial intelligence" is held at Dartmouth College.

1957 An IBM team introduces FORTRAN, the first widely successful programming language.

The romantic comedy *Desk Set*, starring Katherine Hepburn and Spencer Tracy, playfully deals with the public anxiety about computers replacing human workers.

1958 The integrated circuit, or computer on a

chip, is demonstrated. It opens the door to rapid advances in computing.

Software is first used as a computer term.

1961 MIT demonstrates technology that allows many users to share a computer at once, called time-sharing.

1962 Steve Russell, a young programmer at MIT, writes the first interactive computer game, "Spacewar."

Stanford and Purdue establish the first university departments of computer science.

1963 Ivan Sutherland, an MIT graduate student, creates Sketchpad, the first drawing program, a breakthrough in computer graphics.

1964 The computer mouse, invented by Douglas Engelbart, is demonstrated.

BASIC (Beginner's All-purpose Symbolic Instruction Code), an easy-to-use programming language, is introduced on Dartmouth's time-sharing system.

The IBM 360 mainframe, the workhorse of business computing for decades, is introduced.

DIGITAL REVOLUTIONARIES

1965 Gordon Moore, cofounder of Intel, correctly predicts that computer-processing power can double every two years for decades. His observation becomes known as Moore's Law.

1969 The U.S. Defense Department funds a research computer network, Arpanet, which is the seed that becomes the Internet.

1971 The first e-mail message is sent over the Arpanet.

1972 "Pong," the first commercial video game, is released by Atari.

1973 The Xerox Palo Alto Research Center shows off the Alto, a prototype personal computer.

1974 Charles Simonyi, a researcher at Xerox PARC, writes the first graphical word-processing program, which becomes the basis for Microsoft Word.

1975 The MITS Altair 8800, an inexpensive computer kit, is released.

Microsoft introduces its first product, Microsoft BASIC, for the Altair.

1976 Apple Computer introduces its first product, the Apple I.

1979 VisiCalc, the first spreadsheet program for personal computers, is introduced.

1981 IBM enters the personal computer business, bringing the fledgling PC industry into the mainstream. Microsoft supplies the operating system for the IBM PC.

1982 The personal computer takes *Time* magazine's man-of-the-year award as the "Machine of the Year."

Disney releases the sci-fi film *Tron*, a pioneering computer-graphics movie.

The term *cyberspace* is coined by William Gibson in a short story, *Burning Chrome*.

1984 Apple introduces the Macintosh, the first affordable machine that employs point-and-click computing with a mouse and on-screen graphic icons.

1988 A Cornell graduate student shows the security weaknesses of computer networks by releasing a worm program that clogs the Internet within hours.

DIGITAL REVOLUTIONARIES

1990 Tim Berners-Lee, an English programmer, writes the basic software for the World Wide Web.

Kodak introduces the DCS 100, the first commercially available digital camera.

1991 Linus Torvalds, a Finnish programmer, releases the code for Linux, a free operating system.

1993 The White House goes online with its own Web site.

1994 Netscape Communications, a Silicon Valley start-up, releases the first commercial browser software for easily navigating the Web.

1995 Pixar releases *Toy Story*, the first feature-length movie that is entirely computer generated.

1996 Larry Page and Sergey Brin, graduate students at Stanford, begin work on an Internet search engine, called BackRub, later renamed Google.

1997 IBM's chess-playing computer, Deep Blue, defeats the reigning world champion, Gary Kasparov.

TIMELINE

1998 Web logs, or blogs, where authors not only write posts but also invite reader comments, begin to appear.

First ring tones sold to cell phone customers, in Finland.

2000 January 1, 2000, arrives without the predicted catastrophes, such as plane crashes and power blackouts, resulting from the Y2K millennium software bug.

2001 Apple introduces the first of its iPod digital media players.

2003 Digital cameras outsell film cameras for the first time.

Apple introduces the iTunes Music Store, proving that online music sales will work as a legal alternative to digital piracy.

MySpace social-networking Web site begins, and soon becomes extremely popular, especially with teenagers.

2004 Mark Zuckerberg, a Harvard student, begins Facebook, a social-networking Web site, initially for college students.

DIGITAL REVOLUTIONARIES

2005 First YouTube video, *Me at the Zoo*, showing visit of cofounder Jawed Karim to the San Diego Zoo, is uploaded.

2007 Apple releases the iPhone, a gesture-sensitive touch-screen cell phone with many of the online features of a personal computer.

The Queen of England launches *The Royal Channel* on YouTube, becoming the world's first monarch with a YouTube channel.

2008 With the votes counted, President-elect Barack Obama sends out a three-sentence message on the micro-blogging service, Twitter. "We just made history....Thanks."

Articles

Mechanical "Brain" Is Given to Science

Giant Electronic Calculator Built by IBM, Can Do in Days What Once Took a Lifetime

WILLIAM L. LAURENCE   January 13, 1948

A new gigantic calculating machine, known as the IBM Selective Sequence Electronic Calculator was dedicated yesterday for the use of science. Thomas J. Watson, president of the International Business Machines Corporation, officiated at the affair in the presence of representatives of science, education, government, and business, at the company's headquarters, 590 Madison Avenue.

The new machine, it was said, combines "the speed of the electronic circuits" with "a memory capacity" and the necessary control to utilize this speed and capacity on "the most complex problems of science in institutions of learning, in government, and industry."

In many respects, it was said, the new machine follows the patterns of man's mind in performing sequences of complex calculations. It reads numbers involved in the problem and the instruction that have been prepared for its solution. It consults its own reference tables containing the results of previous calculations.

The memory element retains the many intermediate results accumulated within the machine and recalls them when they are required in subsequent phases of the calculations. The calculating element adds, subtracts, multiplies, divides, and can do square and cube roots.

By means of a "central nervous system," the program devised by the scientist for solution of a problem automatically directs the sequence of operations, selects the proper numbers from the various memory units or from the reference table, directs them to the calculating unit, guides the calculating processes, and routes the results back to their proper places in the memory unit.

When the desired results are obtained, the program directs the machine to record them.

Parts Run to Many Thousands

The machine contains 12,500 electronic tubes, 21,400 relays, and 40,000 pluggable connections. Its storage (memory) capacity is 400,000 digits in tubes, relays, and punched tapes. Its reading speed from punched tapes is 140,000 digits a minute, from punched cards, 30,000 digits a minute. There are sixty-six tape reading units and two card-reading units.

Science, government, and industry will benefit from the versatility and efficiency of the new calculator, an IBM announcement said. Instead of spending lifetimes on single problems, as many scientists have been obliged to do, only a few days or months may be required with the new mechanical "brain," and the problems heretofore avoided as being hopelessly time-consuming now can be undertaken.

"The versatility of this powerful mathematics machine," the IBM announcement declared, "makes it applicable in all fields of physical science, both pure and applied, and the social sciences as well."

Theoretical physics, including atomic developments, is another field that offers a multitude of mathematical problems requiring calculations of almost inconceivable magnitude and complexity.

IBM scientists and engineers who collaborated in producing the machine include Dr. W. H. Eckert, who will serve as director of the research program being planned for the calculator; F. E. Hamilton, senior engineer, who directed design, construction, and assembly, and R. R. Seeber Jr., who supervised the functional and operating features and served as liaison between engineering and scientific groups.

Others included H. J. Klotz, R. A. Rowley, B. E. Phelps, J. J. Troy, E. S. Hughes, R. W. Prentice, G. E. Mitchell, T. D. Korayne, P. E. Fox, C. S. Jackoski, and O. L. Hibbard.

Development of the electronic arithmetical unit is the product of several years of work by J. W. Bryce, A. H. Dickinson, C. A. Bergfors, R. L Palmer and B. E. Phelps. The multi-circuit pluggable relays, as well as the contral panels, were designed and developed by C. D. Lake and W. Pfaff.

Computing would not have become what it is today without necessary advances in the field of electronics, and the development of the transistor was one of the first to lead the way.

Tiny Tube Excites Electronics Field

Experts See "Transistor," Size of Corn Kernel, as Basis of Giant New Industry

January 13, 1952

A tiny crystal device called the transistor, about the size of a kernel of corn, has electronics engineers and military men excited over its vast potentials. Some rate it as one of the most important developments in electronics since the vacuum tube, which made possible the modern telephone, radio, television, radar and countless other electronics marvels, according to the Associated Press.

The transistor can do many of the things a vacuum tube can do; it can do some better. Besides being a fraction of the size of a vacuum tube, it's many times as rugged, takes only a minute amount of electricity, requires no warm-up before starting to operate, and—having no filament to burn out—will last indefinitely.

The transistor, first developed by Bell Telephone laboratories in 1948 and greatly improved since then, will go into first practical use in about a year in long distance telephone equipment. Other early applications may be in tubeless radios, smaller, more efficient hearing aids that will work for a year without a change of batteries, and in your telephone set so that you can hear and be heard clearly and loudly even on the remotest rural line.

Seen Promoting Giant Industry

But even greater things are

expected of the transistor in making possible the application of electronics for many uses now impossible with the vacuum tube. Robert M. Burns, chemical director of Bell Laboratories, foresees a new electronics industry based on the transistor that "will become the only rival in size of the chemical industry, that growing industrial group that seems destined to take over all other manufacturing industry.

"The principle operating industries, electric power, transportation and communications, will continue to depend equally upon the electronic and chemical industries" he declares. "So we may look ahead to the time when the electron will do man's work, including thinking, while chemistry supplies him with food, clothing and everything else."

The transistor was invented by Dr. William Shockley, of Bell Laboratories. The first model consisted of two tiny wires pressed against a speck of germanium, a substance belonging to a family of materials known as semi-conductors. They are enclosed in a metal cylinder about the size of a 22-calibre rifle bullet.

Last July, the laboratories announced a radically new type called a junction transistor.

It consists of a tiny piece of germanium treated so that it provides a thin electrically positive layer sandwiched between two electrically negative layers, with wires connected to each layer. It is inside a tiny plastic case and takes up only one-fiftieth the space of a typical sub-miniature vacuum tube. With the wires protruding, the device resembles a spider.

One Bell System publication, in assaying the potentials of the transistor, points out its application in mathematical computing machines—the fabulous "electronic brains." Despite the massive amounts of calculations they can accomplish, the publication said, "present machines boast about one-millionth of man's mental power; but, according to at least one scientist, transistors can increase this by a hundred thousand fold."

In 1967, the creator of the FORTRAN programming language walked readers through a programming simulation. Then, as now, the trick was to understand how a computer thinks—in simple, concrete steps.

3 . . . 2 . . . 1 . . . You Are a Computer, You Can Learn How to Program Yourself as Easy as ABD . . . or Something.

JOHN W. BACKUS   January 9, 1967

Programming is the art of getting a computer to perform a task by breaking down the task into a repetitive sequence of simpler ones. To understand more fully what this means the reader is invited to become a computer for the next few moments and actually execute a program.

The program below suggests how a computer might be told to look up the word IT in any alphabetically arranged list of words, use the sample below or make up a list of your own.

The trick in being a computer is to perform each successive step of the program exactly as directed. Even though the step has been done before, it should be treated as a new step since it will refer to new things.

SAMPLE DATA
(A List in Alphabetical Order)

A
COMPUTERS
I
INTERESTS
IT
NOT
ONE
WHIT

PROGRAM

1. Circle the first letter of the first word in the list. Go to step 2.

2. Does the circled letter come before "I" in the alphabet? If the answer is "yes," cross out the old circled letter, put a circle around the first letter of the next word and then repeat step 2; if the answer is "no," go on to step 3.

3. Is the circled letter "I"? If the answer is "yes," go on to step 4; if the answer is "no," go to step 7.

4. Is there another letter in the same word following the circled letter? If the answer is "yes," cross out the circled letter, circle the next letter in the same word and go on to step 5; if the answer is "no," cross out the circled letter, circle the first letter of the next word and go back to step 3.

5. Does the circled letter come before "T" in the alphabet? If the answer is "yes," cross out the circled letter, circle the first letter of the next word and go back to step 3; if the answer is "no," go on to step 6.

6. Is the circled letter "T" and is it the last letter of the word? If the answer is "yes," the word is IT and the reader has successfully completed a brief but monotonous career as a computer. If the answer is "no," go to step 7.

7. If this step is reached, then one of the following applies:

    (a)   IT is not in the list

    (b)   The list is not in alphabetical order

    (c)   The computer goofed, that is, the reader made some error in one of the steps. The order in which letters of the sample data should have been circled is: A, C, I, I, N, I, T.

                    or

    (d)   The programmer goofed, that is, the author made some error in the program.

The reader may think this program is inefficient, and in a way it is, because it inspects every word that precedes IT, no matter how many there are in the list. People, when searching for IT in the dictionary, do not inspect every previous word; rather, they estimate its approximate position in the dictionary, look there, and—based on the section of the alphabet they opened to—estimate again how much farther on or farther back to look. This process is repeated (usually less than 12 times) until the word is found.

A very fast list-searching program could be written to imitate the human method, but it would take much more work to write than the simple program above. The fast program would need steps telling the computer whether to move forward or backward in the list, how to estimate how far to move, and so on.

Right Balance Needed

The choice between the fast but complicated program and the slow but simpler one is ultimately one of economics: The fast program is cheaper to use since it needs less computer time, but it is more expensive to program since it is more complicated.

If very much list-searching is needed, the fast program will probably be more economical; if only a few lists are to be searched, the slow one might be cheaper. It is often difficult to decide between the two extremes.

Many programs used in the industry cost tens, even hundreds, of thousands of dollars to produce. Programming managers face enormous difficulties balancing cost and speed.

In addition to the speed-economy problem, there are other difficulties, and consequent costs, that arise from an unfortunate characteristic of computers—their absolutely staggering stupidity.

For example, one step in the above program tells the computer to decide whether a certain letter is "T" or not. If, when executing the step, the computer, through some error, got a number instead of a letter, it would not print, "Hey, you idiot, you gave me a number instead of a letter!"

Instead, it might blithely decide that the number was "T" and continue as if nothing were wrong.

No Distinction Made

It can make this error because all the data, both letters and numbers, are represented in the computer as sequences of zeroes and ones, and a number could be represented the same way "T" was. It is the programmer who must make sure that number data are processed only by steps appropriate for numbers, and letter data by steps appropriate for letters.

The stupidity of computers makes it necessary to anticipate and provide for every situation that can occur when using a program. The skill and time-consuming care required to attempt to do this are themselves costly.

Moreover, even the best programmers make mistakes. And when they do, a lot of expensive machine time has to be used before the mistake can be found and corrected.

For example, the above program provides for a variety of possibilities in step 7, such as the omission of IT from the list. But there is at least one mistake, or bug in the program, one situation it is not prepared for.

Suppose a computer by some chance was given only the first four words of the sample list. After reaching INTERESTS and looking at its first two letters, the computer is told to direct its attention to the first letter of the next word. But there is no next word.

The stupid computer, however, will not know this and will pick up whatever is stored where the "next word" would have been had there been one. Whether the computer picks up as its next word a blank or a number used in an earlier program, it will continue on its crazy course until it thinks it has found IT or hangs up at step 7.

In either case, the chaos that results may make it very difficult to discover what went wrong.

To make programming less difficult and computers less likely to make mistakes, computers have been equipped with programming systems that, by using a special language adapted to the needs of the user, enable engineers, scientists, businessmen and scholars to use computers without knowing much about them

In other words, programming systems let people use computers without having to write the thousands of very detailed machine instructions a computer needs to execute a program. A physicist, for example, by using a special programming language, which he can learn easily, can program a complicated calculation in only a few dozen steps. However, the physicist's program cannot be directly executed by the computer.

A Program's Program

As usual, another program, belonging to the programming system, will have to tell the computer how to interpret and carry out the steps the physicist has written.

Programming systems are often designed to handle particular types of calculations.

For example, ALGOL (Algorithmic Language) FORTRAN (Formula Translator) and MAD (Michigan Algorithm Recorder) are systems primarily designed for scientific and engineering calculations. Their source languages provide convenient notations for describing elaborate computations with large sets of numbers. Other systems, such as COMIT (Computing System M.I.T.) and SNOBOL (String Oriented Symbolic Language) deal with natural languages or other texts of letters and words.

Another important type of system is aimed at the areas of accounting, record-keeping and many other tasks useful in running a business. The system COBOL (Common Oriented Business Language), which was government sponsored, is the most widely used system for business applications.

By anticipating the needs of their users, programming systems often reduce the programming effort to one-tenth of what was needed to do a specific job. And since the programming cost is a large proportion of the total cost, the development of standard programming systems has effected great economies.

More important, without the programming systems that enable nonprofessionals to use them, the wide use of computers—which is revolutionizing the world—could never have occurred.

With the introduction of floppy disks, computer users were able for the first time to store data outside of the computer. Floppy sales skyrocketed in the early 1980s, paving the way for 3-inch disks, CD-ROMs, and flash drives.

The Floppy Disk Comes of Age

WILLIAM BATES   December 10, 1978

Los Angeles—the floppy disk and its associated drive, once ugly ducklings among computer technologies, have suddenly come into their own this year—and there are indications that a new version due out in 1979 may make the past mere prologue. Some analysts see the floppy as a candidate to be the cornerstone of the office of the future. Two signs of its rejuvenation: a new popularity in the consumer market and the entry of Xerox into the fold.

The floppy stores information, serving as magnetic "memory" for typewriters and word-processing devices. Its drive is to the disk what a record-player is to a record. This year sales of disks—which typically cost $5 to $8 apiece—are expected to reach $135 million, up from $96 million in 1977; sales of the disk drives, which were $289.6 million last year, are expected to increase by about 75 percent.

Most of the million floppy disks sold each month still move through traditional industry distribution channels for data-processing supplies, but this year they have begun invading such odd outlets for computer supplies as camera shops, department stores and stereo dealers.

And last month, the largest manufacturer of floppy disks, the Information Terminals Corporation of Sunnyvale, Calif., launched an advertising campaign, using Victor Borge to introduce its Verbatim disk.

"The ads are just like ads for soap suds or automobiles," says Rodney E. Crisp, product manager for I.T.C. "We're advertising right to the consumer to create a demand on retailers for our product." The particular consumers I.T.C. has in mind are such record-keepers as doctors, lawyers, and small businessmen.

Competing with Paper

"Floppy" as a description of the disks is not, actually, quite accurate; they really only droop. They are thin, Mylar platters, 8 inches in diameter in the standard size; the minifloppy is 5¼ inches in diameter. The surface of each disk—where the grooves would be on a phonograph record of the same size—is smooth and coated with a magnetic oxide similar to that used in recording tape. This surface is protected from fingerprints and scratches with a square paper envelope.

The product is surprisingly cheap and tough. In manufacturing cost the price of the disks approaches that of audio cassettes. I.T.C., which has approximately 35 percent of the estimated $135 million floppy disk market—which it expects to see rise to $235 million by 1981—sells the minifloppy disks in large quantities for $1.50.

At these prices floppy disks have begun to compete with an item found in abundance in offices—paper. The secret lies in the tremendous quantities of information that can be magnetically recorded on the floppy disk's surface—over a quarter-million typewritten characters on today's standard 8-inch disk. Newer disks, which record at double the density of the old, and on both sides, have increased this capacity by a factor of four, making it possible to place no fewer than 300 pages of manuscript on a single $8 disk.

This type of data capacity can be found in other computer devices—notably in the floppy disk's cousin, the so-called "hard" disk. But unlike the floppy, which can, within reason, be bent and otherwise manhandled out of shape—expensive hard disks can be ruined if their metal cylinders are dropped or dented. Older versions of the hard disk require air-conditioning and air filtration, and can be stopped dead by cigarette smoke, or even heavy perfume. The floppy, by contrast, faces up far better to office hazards.

Says Stuart Mabon, president of Micropolis, a Canoga Park, Calif., manufacturer of floppy-disk drives popular in word-processing applications, "You can almost spill coffee on them."

The real money in the floppy technology, of course, is not so much with the disks as with the drives. They resemble a bizarre cross between the phonograph and tape recorder, with a moving recording head, similar to the recording head of the tape recorder, taking the place of the needle that moves across the tracks of the record. Stranger still is the fact that the floppy disk, unlike a phonograph record, never leaves its protective paper envelope—the recording head reaches the floppy disk's surface through a small slot in the paper, while the disk whirs, often noisily, inside.

High volume manufacturers, like the Xerox-owned Shugart Associates of Sunnyvale, Calif., are beginning to manufacture the minifloppy drives in quantities that resemble those of its consumer electronics relatives. The minifloppy drive is available to volume buyers, like Fort Worth's Tandy Corporation, parent of Radio Shack chain, at approximately $165 each, and sell to end customers for about $500. Shugart is beginning, but only beginning, to gain market share on I.B.M., which makes only standard-size drives, sells them at higher prices and has approximately one-third of the market measured by revenue.

The Xerox Corporation got into the business last December when it traded some $41 million worth of its stock for Shugart, a company that pioneered the minifloppy drive. Shugart's sales had climbed from $18 million in the fiscal year ended last spring.

The acquisition may give Xerox some advantages in the rapidly growing word-processing area. One Xerox typing system, manufactured in Dallas, already uses Shugart's full-sized floppy disk drives, and other floppy-based products are expected from the company soon. I.B.M., for its part, seems to be concentrating its efforts on bubble-memory technology, which, when perfected, could provide a typewriter with a cheap, built-in memory capable of playing back several pages of text. This technology uses tiny magnetic domains, or bubbles, in a silicon chip to permanently store information. But since the discovery of the technology of a decade ago, commercial development has been slow.

The American Telephone and Telegraph Company has commissioned studies of both the floppy and the bubble memory as possible information storage devices for an advanced network for business communication.

"They're all positioning themselves to participate in the office-of-the-future environment," says Ulric Weil, an analyst with the investment banking firm of Morgan Stanley. "Every work station in the future will have a floppy disk or bubble memory."

Laboratory versions of the floppy have been in existence since 1960, but the first commercial floppy did not come on the market until 1971—and then as an accessory to one of I.B.M's major hard-disk units.

The next year, however, the floppy got its break, when I.B.M., in a search to replace its aging fleet of keypunch machines, picked the floppy out of a chorus line of competing technologies to take the part of its infamous punch cards. I.B.M. announced its floppy-based keypunch replacement machine, the 3741, in August 1972.

"It was like a flashbulb going off," recalls Al Shugart, one of the founders of Shugart Associates, which he left in 1973. "I.B.M.'s announcement of the 3741 was the stamp of approval for the medium. It was all anybody needed to get going."

In the original data-entry version, each 8-inch floppy was designed to hold the equivalent of 3,000 punch cards—a number judged by I.B.M. engineers to be the maximum possible for a single operator to produce in one day.

The floppy, however, had far more capacity than was required for this operation—and in recent years, led by small-business users, including businessmen who now keep their entire sales and inventory records on a collection of floppy disks—engineers have begun recording data on floppy disks at twice the density used in the I.B.M. format, and on both sides of the disk, thereby increasing the capacity of the floppy by a factor of four.

For the standard 8-inch disk, these improvements put the amount of information a single floppy can hold at well above one "megabite"—the equivalent of a million typewritten characters. The double-sided disks, announced this year, have had production difficulties and will not hit the market in quantity until 1979. When they do, however, some industry observers expect the floppy market to boil over.

"I think one megabite is going to prove to be a magic number in this industry," says George Morrow, whose company, Morrow's Microstuff of Berkeley, Calif., recently announced a $995 one-megabite disk drive. "Everybody and their brother are going to decide that now is the time to switch to floppy disks.

They're going to come up from tape and down from disks and turn the floppy into the wildest product you ever saw."

In some respects, the market for floppy disks is already quite wild. Shugart, which is easily the industry leader in volume, now moves some 1,200 floppy disk drives off its line each day—a production level in the low range of that found in consumer electronics manufacturing.

According to a Mountain View, Calif., management consultant, James N. Porter, whose Disk/Trend report is the standard source of statistics in the industry, sales of the 8-inch floppy drives will be up this year by some 54 percent from 1977. He expects revenue to makers of all sizes of floppy-disk drives to increase from $289.6 million in 1977 to some $875 million by 1981.

How did the computer mouse evolve? This article gives a glimpse into its early development.

A Big 1983 Expected for the Digital Mouse

ERIK SANDBERG-DIMENT   December 7, 1982

Having run through apples, oranges, limes, peaches, and most of the other familiar fruits in search of people-comforting nomenclature, personal computing marketers are now setting their sight on animals. Witness, for instance, Leading Edge's Elephant floppy disks. However, the biggest computer news personality of all is soon to be the pachyderm's mythological archenemy, the mouse. In fact, after visiting the Comdex computer conference and exposition in Las Vegas last week, I came away with very much the feeling that 1983 will see the ascendancy of the digital mouse.

There were mice all over the Convention Center—not among the neon-flashing, balloon-frosted displays of new comput-

ers, disk drives, and tantalizing graphics systems, but scurrying about beneath the tables and in the hidden boxes backstage of the booths. What with so many firms trying to be both first to the cheese and secretive to the end at the same time, the marketing strategy in evidence seemed to parallel the psychology of *Mus musculus* itself.

Mice as data-entry devices actually first entered the world of computers back in 1967 when Douglas Engelbart fathered the first potentiometer-driven rodent. Eventually a soap-bar-size box with a couple of buttons for ears and a long tail connecting it to the computer, this device measured changes in electrical potential as it was pushed back and forth. Using analog, rather than digital, technology, the mouse's movements had to be translated into computer-intelligible information before a person, or a pointer, could be shifted back and forth across the display on the computer's monitor screen. Even so, cursor direction could be controlled without the operator having to use the keyboard.

While it may not seem much of an accomplishment, a mouse coupled to the right software makes accessible a whole new style of computing. Instead of dealing with Cartesian coordinates, requiring the computer operator to strike the cursor keys, say, seventeen times for left and twelve for up, all that need be done to reach a desired location on the screen is to move the mouse so that the cursor sidles directly into the appropriate division, traveling with ease even diagonally.

Essentially, mice allow a nonverbal expression of information. You can say "Put it here" by merely pointing, rather than by typing in the commands. Touch screens had also emerged by the time mice appeared. But fingers are larger than the small points composing a video image, and you can't see through them. Besides, they leave greasy fingerprints. Light pens, besides being clumsy, pose the same problem of obstruction, minus the fingerprints. Joysticks can be used for cursor movement. However, they don't leave the hand free to press the command or function keys for actually inducing the computer to perform the desired tasks.

Despite the evolutionary advance they represented, mice remained confined to the laboratories for a number of years, breeding but slowly, until Jack S. Hawley developed the first digital mouse for Xerox in 1972. The digital mouse and today's computers are very cozy. Both speak the same binary electronic language of ones and zeroes, on and off, plus and minus.

Known as the Alto Mouse, Mr. Hawley's rodent was used internally at Xerox for quite some time. It finally escaped into the world at large attached to Xerox's Star computer system. But at some $20,000 or so for the complete Star system, the electronic mouse was not about to join the biological original in most people's homes.

Meanwhile, however, Hawley opened the Mouse House, with the slogan "Purveyors of Fine Digital Mice to an Exclusive Clientele Since 1975," in Berkeley, Calif., and set about building a better mouse for which the world would beat a path to his door. His current mouse is called X063X—you were expecting maybe Mickey? Manufactured under license from Xerox, it uses a ball on its bottom to sense movement and direction. Essentially, it's an upside-down trackball, like those used on many video arcade games. On top are three buttons which permit the operator to activate various functions, such as text selection, scrolling and graphics manipulation, while still palming the mouse.

Other companies, such as U.S.I International of Brisbane, Calif., and Mouse Systems of Corporation, in Sunnyvale, Calif., produce optical mice bearing names like Optomouse and M-I. These rodent renegades from some hybrid opthalmological world use a special grid as their turf. An optical mouse pushed back and forth across a special typewriter-paper-sized board optically senses the grid beneath its feet and translates its motion into digital impulses.

Proponents of optical mice claim they are superior to mechanical ones because they have no moving parts to break down and no ball to become gummed up. The advocates of mechanical mice, on the other hand, feel that the need for a special pad upon which the optical mouse will dance limits its flexibility.

The first battle of the mouse war has only begun. It may turn out that neither optical nor mechanical mice will prove to be the eventual winners. For as the Pied Piper of personal computing begins to play the consumers' tune, a whole host of mice are beginning to clamber out of the growth and circuit cellar of Silicon Valley. Most of the new rodents can be expected to sell in the $100 to $200 range, with software extra. As usual in the industry, the little black boxes are preceding the content, and so the game of software catch-up will start all over again.

But for starters, Visicorp, producer of the now-legendary Visicalc software for financial modeling, has announced its new Vision, a mouse-manipulated program that reduces operator learning time to a fraction of that formerly required for Visicalc and comparable programs. At the same time, Vision integrates a whole host of related programs and graphics into one. It's like having a desk covered with paper to shuffle. The computer screen is divided into a number of overlapping "windows," and you use the mouse to move the cursor over to the sheet, or window, you want, press an ear, and the sheet moves to the fore. Move the mouse so that the cursor goes to any of the command words, such as "Phase," "Transfer" or the crucial "Help," press an ear and the computer does what you want it to do.

Vision (with mouse) is expected to be available for most of the newer personal computers by the summer of 1983. Apple is rumored to be bringing out a mouse even sooner. Its much-awaited McIntosh should be in the stores by early spring. The new-generation Apple will be priced competitively with the Apple II. And what goes better with Apples than cheese?

The increase in processing power has created computers that are millions of times more powerful than those available to researchers in the 1960s when Artificial Intelligence was first explored, making the possibility of intelligent computer devices for consumer use a real possibility.

Brainy Robots Start Stepping Into Daily Life

JOHN MARKOFF   July 18, 2006

Robot cars drive themselves across the desert, electronic eyes perform lifeguard duty in swimming pools and virtual enemies with humanlike behavior battle video game players.

These are some fruits of the research field known as artificial intelligence, where reality is finally catching up to the science-fiction hype. A half-century after the term was coined, both scientists and engineers say they are making rapid progress in simulating the human brain, and their work is finding its way into a new wave of real-world products.

The advances can also be seen in the emergence of bold new projects intended to create more ambitious machines that can improve safety and security, entertain and inform, or just handle everyday tasks. At Stanford University, for instance, computer scientists are developing a robot that can use a hammer and a screwdriver to assemble an Ikea bookcase (a project beyond the reach of many humans) as well as tidy up after a party, load a dishwasher or take out the trash.

One pioneer in the field is building an electronic butler that could hold a conversation with its master—á la HAL in the movie "2001: A Space Odyssey"—or order more pet food.

Though most of the truly futuristic projects are probably years from the commercial market, scientists say that after a lull, artificial intelligence has rapidly grown far more sophisticated. Today some scientists are beginning to use the term cognitive computing to distinguish their research from an earlier generation of artificial intelligence work. What sets the new researchers apart is a wealth of new biological data on how the human brain functions.

"There's definitely been a palpable upswing in methods, competence and boldness," said Eric Horvitz, a Microsoft researcher who is president-elect of the American Association for Artificial Intelligence. "At conferences you are hearing the phrase 'human-level A.I.,' and people are saying that without blushing."

Cognitive computing is still more of a research discipline than an industry that can be measured in revenue or profits. It is pursued in various pockets of academia and the business world. And despite some of the more startling achievements, improvements in the field are measured largely in increments: voice recognition systems with decreasing failure rates, or computerized cameras that can recognize more faces and objects than before.

Still, there have been rapid innovations in many areas: voice control systems are now standard features in midpriced automobiles, and advanced artificial reason techniques are now routinely used in inexpensive video games to make the characters' actions more lifelike.

A French company, Poseidon Technologies, sells underwater vision systems for swimming pools that function as lifeguard assistants, issuing alerts when people are drowning, and the system has saved lives in Europe.

Last October, a robot car designed by a team of Stanford engineers covered 132 miles of desert road without human intervention to capture a $2 million prize offered by the Defense Advanced Research Projects Agency, part of the Pentagon. The feat was particularly striking because 18 months earlier, during the first such competition, the best vehicle got no farther than seven miles, becoming stuck after driving off a mountain road.

Now the Pentagon agency has upped the ante: Next year the robots will be back on the road, this time in a simulated traffic setting. It is being called the "urban challenge."

At Microsoft, researchers are working on the idea of "predestination." They envision a software program that guesses where you are traveling based on previous trips, and then offers information that might be useful based on where the software thinks you are going.

Tellme Networks, a company in Mountain View, Calif., that provides voice recognition services for both customer service and telephone directory applications, is a good indicator of the progress that is being made in relatively constrained situations, like looking up a phone number or transferring a call.

Tellme supplies the system that automates directory information for toll-free business listings. When the service was first introduced in 2001, it could correctly answer fewer than 37 percent of phone calls without a human operator's help. As the system has been constantly refined, the figure has now risen to 74 percent.

More striking advances are likely to come from new biological models of the brain. Researchers at the École Polytechnique Fédérale de Lausanne in Lausanne, Switzerland, are building large-scale computer models to study how the brain works; they have used an I.B.M. parallel supercomputer to create the most detailed three-dimensional model to date of a column of 10,000 neurons in the neocortex.

"The goal of my lab in the past 10 to 12 years has been to go inside these little columns and try to figure out how they are built with exquisite detail," said Henry Markram, a research scientist who is head of the Blue Brain project. "You can really now zoom in on single cells and watch the electrical activity emerging."

Blue Brain researchers say they believe the simulation will provide fundamental insights that can be applied by scientists who are trying to simulate brain functions.

Another well-known researcher is Robert Hecht-Nielsen, who is seeking to build an electronic butler called Chancellor that would be able to listen, speak, and provide in-home concierge services. He contends that with adequate resources, he could create such a machine within five years.

Although some people are skeptical that Mr. Hecht-Nielsen can achieve what he describes, he does have one successful artificial intelligence business under his belt. In 1986, he founded HNC Software, which sold systems to detect credit card fraud using neural network technology designed to mimic biological circuits in the brain. HNC was sold in 2002 to the Fair Isaac Corporation, where Mr. Hecht-Nielsen is a vice president and leads a small research group.

Last year he began speaking publicly about his theory of "confabulation," a hypothesis about the way the brain makes decisions. At a recent I.B.M. symposium, Mr. Hecht-Nielsen showed off a model of confabulation, demonstrating how his software program could read two sentences from *The Detroit Free Press* and create a third sentence that both made sense and was a natural extension of the previous text.

For example, the program read: "He started his goodbyes with a morning audience with Queen Elizabeth II at Buckingham Palace, sharing coffee, tea, cookies, and his desire for a golf rematch with her son, Prince Andrew. The visit came after Clinton made the rounds through Ireland and Northern Ireland to offer support for the flagging peace process there."

The program then generated a sentence that read: "The two leaders also discussed bilateral cooperation in various fields."

Artificial intelligence had its origins in 1950, when the mathematician Alan Turing proposed a test to determine whether or not a machine could think or be conscious. The test involved having a person face two teleprinter machines, only one of which had a human behind it. If the human judge could not tell which terminal was controlled by the human, the machine could be said to be intelligent.

In the late 1950s a field of study emerged that tried to build systems that replicated human abilities like speech, hearing, manual tasks and reasoning.

During the 1960s and 1970s, the original artificial intelligence researchers began designing computer software programs they called "expert systems," which were essentially databases accompanied by a set of logical rules. They were handicapped both by underpowered computers and by the absence of the wealth of data that today's researchers have amassed about the actual structure and function of the biological brain.

Those shortcomings led to the failure of a first generation of artificial intelligence companies in the 1980s, which became known as the A.I. Winter. Recently, however, researchers have begun to speak of an A.I. Spring emerging as scientists develop theories on the workings of the human mind. They are being aided by the exponential increase in processing power, which has created computers with millions of times the power of those available to researchers in the 1960s—at consumer prices.

"There is a new synthesis of four fields, including mathematics, neuroscience, computer science and psychology," said Dharmendra S. Modha, an I.B.M. computer scientist. "The implication of this is amazing. What you are seeing is that cognitive computing is at a cusp where it's knocking on the door of potentially mainstream applications."

At Stanford, researchers are hoping to make fundamental progress in mobile robotics, building machines that can carry out tasks around the home, like the current generation of robotic floor vacuums, only more advanced. The field has recently been dominated by Japan and South Korea, but the Stanford researchers have sketched out a three-year plan to bring the United States to parity.

At the moment, the Stanford team is working on the first steps necessary to make the robot they are building function well in an American household. The team is focusing on systems that will consistently recognize standard doorknobs and is building robot hands to open doors.

"It's time to build an A.I. robot," said Andrew Ng, a Stanford computer scientist and a leader of the project, called Stanford Artificial Intelligence Robot, or Stair. "The dream is to put a robot in every home."

Future trends in computer imaging and storing, along with social-and-technology networks were discussed by computer scientists from academia and business at a symposium called "2016."

Computing, 2016: What Won't Be Possible?

STEVE LOHR   October 31, 2006

Computer science is not only a comparatively young field, but also one that has had to prove it is really science. Skeptics in academia would often say that after Alan Turing described the concept of the "universal machine" in the late 1930s—the idea that a computer in theory could be made to do the work of any kind of calculating machine, including the human brain—all that remained to be done was mere engineering.

The more generous perspective today is that decades of stunningly rapid advances in processing speed, storage, and networking, along with the development of increasingly clever software, have brought computing into science, business, and culture in ways that were barely imagined years ago. The quantitative changes delivered through smart engineering opened the door to qualitative changes.

Computing changes what can be seen, simulated, and done. So in science, computing makes it possible to simulate climate change and unravel the human genome. In business, low-cost computing, the Internet, and digital communications are transforming the global economy. In culture, the artifacts of computing include the iPod, YouTube, and computer-animated movies.

What's next? That was the subject of a symposium in Washington this month held by the Computer Science and Telecommunications Board, which is part of the National Academies and the nation's leading advisory board on science and technology. Joseph F. Traub, the board's chairman and a professor at Columbia University, titled the symposium "2016."

Computer scientists from academia and companies like I.B.M. and Google discussed topics including social networks, digital imaging, online media, and the impact on work and employment. But most talks touched on two broad themes: the impact of computing will go deeper into the sciences and spread more into the social sciences, and policy issues will loom large, as the technology becomes more powerful and more pervasive.

Richard M. Karp, a professor at the University of California, Berkeley, gave a talk whose title seemed esoteric: "The Algorithmic Nature of Scientific Theories."

Yet he presented a fundamental explanation for why computing has had such a major impact on other sciences, and Dr. Karp himself personifies the trend. His research has moved beyond computer science to microbiology in recent years. An algorithm, put simply, is a step-by-step recipe for calculation, and it is a central concept in both mathematics and computer science.

"Algorithms are small but beautiful," Dr. Karp observed. And algorithms are good at describing dynamic processes, while scientific formulas or equations are more suited to static phenomena. Increasingly, scientific research seeks to understand dynamic processes, and computer science, he said, is the systematic study of algorithms.

Biology, Dr. Karp said, is now understood as an information science. And scientists seek to describe biological processes, like protein production, as algorithms. "In other words, nature is computing," he said.

Social networks, noted Jon Kleinberg, a professor at Cornell, are pre-technological creations that sociologists have been analyzing for decades. A classic example, he noted, was the work of the psychologist Stanley Milgram, who in the 1960s asked each of several volunteers in the Midwest to get a letter to a stranger in Boston. But the path was not direct: under the rules of the experiment, participants could send a letter only to someone they knew. The median number of intermediaries was six —hence, the term "six degrees of separation."

But with the rise of the Internet, social networks and technology networks are becoming inextricably linked, so that behavior in social networks can be tracked on a scale never before possible.

"We're really witnessing a revolution in measurement," Dr. Kleinberg said.

The new social-and-technology networks that can be studied include e-mail patterns, buying recommendations on commercial Web sites like Amazon, messages and postings on community sites like MySpace and Facebook, and the diffusion of news, opinions, fads, urban myths, products and services over the Internet. Why do some online communities thrive, while others decline and perish? What forces or characteristics determine success? Can they be captured in a computing algorithm?

Social networking research promises a rich trove for marketers and politicians, as well as sociologists, economists, anthropologists, psychologists, and educators.

"This is the introduction of computing and algorithmic processes into the social sciences in a big way," Dr. Kleinberg said, "and we're just at the beginning."

But having a powerful new tool of tracking the online behavior of groups and individuals also raises serious privacy issues. That became apparent this summer when AOL inadvertently released Web search logs of 650,000 users.

Future trends in computer imaging and storage will make it possible for a person, wearing a tiny digital device with a microphone and camera, to essentially record his or her life. The potential for communication, media, and personal enrichment is striking. Rick Rashid, a computer scientist and head of Microsoft's research labs, noted that he would like to see a recording of the first steps of his grown son, or listen to a conversation he had with his father many years ago. "I'd like some of that back," he said. "In the future, that will be possible."

But clearly, the technology could also enable a surveillance society. "We'll have the capability, and it will be up to society to determine how we use it," Dr. Rashid said. "Society will determine that, not scientists."

Source Notes

The following articles from *The New York Times* appear as images, excerpts, or supplemental text throughout the book:

Page 6: Brown, Patricia Leigh. "Techno-Dwellings for the Cyber-Egos of the Mega-Rich" *The New York Times*, August 4, 1996.

Page 36: Kennedy, Jr., T. R. "Electronic Computer Flashes Answers, May Speed Engineering." *The New York Times*, February 15, 1946.

Page 123: Laurence, William L. "Mechanical 'Brain' Is Given to Science." *The New York Times*, January 28, 1948.

Page 125: "Tiny Tube Excites Electronics Field." *The New York Times*, January 13, 1952.

Page 127: Backus, John W. "3...2...1...You Are a Computer, You Can Learn to Program Yourself as Easily as ABD...or Something." *The New York Times*, January 9, 1967.

Page 132: Bates, William. "The Floppy Disk Comes of Age." *The New York Times*, December 10, 1978.

SOURCE NOTES

Page 137: Sandberg-Diment, Erik. "A Big 1983 Expected for the Digital Mouse." *The New York Times*, December 7, 1982.

Page 141: Markoff, John. "Brainy Robots Start Stepping into Daily Life." *The New York Times*, July 18, 2006.

Page 146: Lohr, Steve. "Computing, 2016: What Won't Be Possible." *The New York Times*, October 31, 2006.

Photo Credits

Further Reading

For a deeper look at some computing topics covered in this books you may enjoy the following resources.

BOOKS

Revolution in the Valley
by Andy Hertzfeld
O'Reilly Media, Incorporated, 2004

Inside Steve's Brain
by Leander Kahney
Portfolio, 2008

Bill and Dave: How Hewlett and Packard Built the World's Greatest Company
by Michael S. Malone
Penguin, 2007

Geeks: How Two Lost Boys Rode the Internet Out of Idaho
by Jon Katz
Bantam Books, 2001

Just for Fun: The Story of an Accidental Revolutionary
by Linus Torvalds and David Diamond
HarperCollins Publishers, 2002

FURTHER READING

WEB SITES AND ELECTRONIC RESOURCES

The Apple Museum
www.theapplemuseum.com

Charles Babbage Institute Center for the History of
Information Technology
www.cbi.umn.edu

Charles Simonyi's space adventure online
www.charlesinspace.com

Computer History Museum[SM]
www.computerhistory.org

The Doug Engelbart Institute
www.dougengelbart.org

IBM Archives
www-03.ibm.com/ibm/history/index.html

PBS's "Triumph of the Nerds"
www.pbs.org/nerds

Smithsonian Encyclopedia, Science &Technology
www.si.edu/Encyclopedia_SI/Science_and_technology

Smithsonian Institution Computer History Collection
www.americanhistory.si.edu/collections/comphist

FURTHER READING

TED Talks: Tim Berners-Lee on the next Web
www.ted.com/talks/tim_berners_lee_on_the_next_
web.html

University of Washington, Department of Computer
Science and Engineering's Career Page
www.cs.washington.edu/WhyCSE

NEW YORK TIMES ARTICLES

The following articles, from the archives of *The New
York Times*, can be accessed at www.nytimes.com:

EARLY HISTORY

Berdiner, Robert. "The Brain Is Not Outmoded." *The
New York Times*, January 23, 1955.

Kennedy, Jr., T. R. "Electronic Computer Flashes
Answers, May Speed Engineering." *The New York
Times*, February 15, 1946.

Lohr, Steve. "The Face of Computing 50 Years and
18,000 Tubes Ago." *The New York Times*, February 19,
1996.

Lohr, Steve. "When Few Knew the Code, They
Changed the Language." *The New York Times*, June
13, 2001.

Plumb, Robert K. "Great Gains Seen in 'Brain' Machine." *The New York Times*, November 18, 1949.

SCIENCE OF COMPUTING
Bernstein, Jeremy. "When the Computer Procreates." *The New York Times*, February 15, 1976.

Johnson, George. "Computing, One Atom at a Time." *The New York Times*, March 27, 2001.

Johnson, George. "King Algorithm: An Oracle Part Man, Part Machine." *The New York Times*, September 23, 2007.

Markoff, John. "So Who's Talking: Human or Machine?" *The New York Times*, November 5, 1991.

Tierney, John. "Technology That Outthinks Us: A Partner or a Master?" *The New York Times*, August 26, 2008.

IMPACT ON CULTURE AND SOCIETY
Gleick, James. "Cyber-Neologoliferation." *The New York Times*, November 5, 2006.

Lohr, Steve. "Slow Down, Brave Multitasker, and Don't Read This in Traffic." *The New York Times*, March 25, 2007.

Lohr, Steve. "Silicon Valley Shaped by Technology and Traffic." *The New York Times*, December 20, 2007.

Rich, Motoko. "In Web Age, Library Job Gets Update." *The New York Times*, February 6, 2009.

Thompson, Clive. "The Making of an Xbox Warrior." *The New York Times*, August 22, 2004.

COMPUTER SECURITY AND PRIVACY

Levy, Steven. "Battle of the Clipper Chip," *The New York Times*, June 12, 1994.

Markoff, John. "Hacker and Grifter Duel on the Net." *The New York Times*, February 19, 1995.

Markoff, John. "How a Need for Challenge Seduced Computer Expert." *The New York Times*, November 6, 1988.

Markoff, John. "You're Leaving a Digital Trail. Should You Care?" *The New York Times*, November 30, 2008.

Thompson, Clive. "The Virus Underground." *The New York Times*, February 8, 2004.

PROFILES

Lohr, Steve. "Creating Jobs." *The New York Times*, January 12, 1997.

FURTHER READING

Lohr, Steve. "His Goal: Keeping the Web Worldwide."
The New York Times, December 18, 1995.

Lohr, Steve. "The PC? That Old Thing? An Industry's
Founding Father Has Better Things to Do." *The New
York Times*, August 18, 2001.

Markoff, John. "I, Robot: The Man Behind the Google
Phone." *The New York Times*, November 4, 2007.

Wade, Nicholas. "Grad Student Becomes Gene Effort's
Unlikely Hero." *The New York Times*, February 13,
2001.

COMPUTING BEYOND COMPUTERS
Markoff, John. "Brainy Robots Start Stepping Into
Daily Life." *The New York Times*, July 18, 2006.

Markoff, John. "The Cellphone, Navigating Our Lives."
The New York Times, February 17, 2009.

IMPACT ON OTHER FIELDS
Lohr, Steve. "A Techie, Absolutely, and More:
Computer Majors Adding Other Skills to Land Jobs."
The New York Times, August 23, 2005.

Lohr, Steve. "Health Care That Puts a Computer on the
Team." *The New York Times*, December 27, 2008.

FURTHER READING

FIRSTHAND VIEWS

Pogue, David. "Apple Waves Its Wand at the Phone."
The New York Times, January 11, 2007.

Pogue, David. "Twitter? It's What You Make It." *The
New York Times*, February 12, 2009.

Schuyten, Peter J. "A Computer to Call Your Own." *The
New York Times*, June 23, 1980.

Acknowledgments

This book is an outgrowth of the reporting opportunities I've had at *The New York Times* for years covering computer technology, the people who build it, and how computing shapes our economy and society. And because the computer is a protean "universal machine," in Alan Turing's phrase, the journey has been continually engaging and fun.

The great appeal of being a journalist is that you get what I think of as a curiosity license—you're free to ask all sorts of questions, and it's your job. Perhaps the best such license in journalism comes with a brand name, *The New York Times*. It opens a lot of doors.

So, just briefly, I'd like to thank a few people at the *Times:* John Lee, who hired me; Max Frankel and Fred Andrews, who graciously allowed me to return to reporting after a brief stint as an editor (following a decade as a foreign correspondent); Joseph Lelyveld, who granted me a leave of absence years ago to write a history of software, *Go To: The Story of the Programmers Who Created the Software Revolution;* and my current editors, Lawrence Ingrassia, Damon Darlin, David Gallagher, and Vindu Goel. And I also owe a debt to my longtime reporting colleague and sounding board, John Markoff.

For this book, there are a few others to thank. At

ACKNOWLEDGMENTS

the *Times:* Alex Ward, who asked me to write the book and suggested an approach; Maggie Berkvist, who was responsible for assembling the photos and artwork; and Tomi Murata, who juggled so many details.

At Roaring Brook Press, Deirdre Langeland shaped the book and was my guide to how to write for younger readers. She edited the book most of the way, and then Andrea Cascardi, another deft editor, came in as the finisher.

This book, of course, never would have been written without the people in it. And I'd like to express my lasting appreciation to these computing technologists and artists for their time, thoughts, and enthusiasm—as well as their contributions to the digital world that increasingly surrounds us.

Index

INDEX

INDEX

Steve Lohr

For more than a decade, Steve Lohr has written about technology and its impact on the economy and society for *The New York Times*. In 1998, he was nominated for a Pulitzer Prize for his coverage of Microsoft and its antitrust battle with the United States Government. He has also written a history of computer programming for adults, *Go To: The Story of the Math Majors, Bridge Players, Engineers, Chess Wizards, Maverick Scientists and Iconoclasts—The Programmers Who Created the Software Revolution*. He lives in New York.